D1552672

Glory

IN THE

MOUNTAINS

THE SOUND OF MANY WATERS

(SECOND EDITION)

Fred B. Lunsford

WESTBOW

PRESS

A DIVISION OF THOMAS NELSON

Copyright © 2010 Fred B. Lunsford

All rights reserved. No part of this book may be used or reproduced by any means, graphic, electronic, or mechanical, including photocopying, recording, taping or by any information storage retrieval system without the written permission of the publisher except in the case of brief quotations embodied in critical articles and reviews.

WestBow Press books may be ordered through booksellers or by contacting:

WestBow Press
A Division of Thomas Nelson
1663 Liberty Drive
Bloomington, IN 47403
www.westbowpress.com
1-(866) 928-1240

Because of the dynamic nature of the Internet, any Web addresses or links contained in this book may have changed since publication and may no longer be valid. The views expressed in this work are solely those of the author and do not necessarily reflect the views of the publisher, and the publisher hereby disclaims any responsibility for them.

Any people depicted in stock imagery provided by Thinkstock are models, and such images are being used for illustrative purposes only.

Certain stock imagery © Thinkstock.

Scripture references are KJV from the Holy Bible: Authorized King James Version.

ISBN: 978-1-4497-0749-1 (sc)
ISBN: 978-1-4497-0751-4 (hc)
ISBN: 978-1-4497-0750-7 (e)
Library of Congress Control Number: 2010939613

Printed in the United States of America

WestBow Press rev. date: 11/02/2010

CONTENTS

Some Memorable Experiences

FOREWORD

By: Dr. Dan G. Lunsford
President of Mars Hill College

The author of this new book delivered in <u>Golden Nuggets from the Mountains</u>, a collection of stories that inspired, reflected on earlier times, and told part of his life story of hard work, family, and faith. For those of us inside the family circle, some were stories we had heard before, while some were new or told more fully than we had remembered. It was especially good for us to see those stories in print, but most significant is the affirming and noteworthy feedback the writer has received.

It is a personal honor to write the introduction for this new book that enhances the first by giving a more in-depth view of the life and ministry of Fred B. Lunsford. The writer has often described himself as "Just a mountain preacher," which is true; but there is much more. This collection is autobiographical in the sense that it tells the stories of the major periods of his life to this point in time, but it has a clear focus on his work in the ministry and how it came to be and was influenced.

The author has been described as "Mr. Baptist of Western North Carolina" during the height of his ministry in the second half of the twentieth century. Yet his life story is the totality of his ministry and life as opposed to the specific stories as they unfolded one by one. As one of two sons of Fred and Gladys Lunsford, I did not realize from inside the family circle the impact of his life and ministry until the stories started coming to me about the impact he has had on so many people. I believe that the readers of this book will be amused at times, inspired for sure, and blessed if they read beyond the words and hear the message of the heart of the writer. I am so pleased that my father has chosen to continue his ministry through the printed word, and I am honored to say, "Well done!"

INTRODUCTION

Through the years, God has blessed me with a wonderful family and now for sixty-five years, the family of my wife, Gladys, as well as many friends, all of which have been a tremendous help to me in my journey with the Lord. I quote again, as I have many times, the words of a great famous singer, Bill Gaither, who said, "If you see a turtle on top of a fence post, you will know that he didn't get there by himself." It is true that so many wonderful people have helped me along the way in doing what God has blessed me to be able to do for His glory. One such person was Dr. Garland Hendrix, who has now gone on to be with the Lord. Dr. Hendrix was a friend for many years. He was a noted author and Bible professor. I was scheduled to speak on one occasion at Shelby, North Carolina. Dr. Hendrix was then professor at Gardner-Webb University. He called me to tell me he was very sorry that he would not be able to be there since he was tied up at the school at that time. When I arrived at the church, the first person I saw standing out front was my friend, Garland Hendrix. I said to him, "I thought you told me you couldn't be here." He replied with that radiant grin with a sparkle in his eye, "I know I told you that, but my want-to took over and I made arrangements to be here. I wanted so very much to hear you."

After the meeting was over, he said to me as he gripped my hand so very firmly while placing his other hand on my shoulder, looking me in the eye with a big crocodile tear trickling down his wrinkled face, "Fred, I love you and you have done it again. You really blessed my heart. Now, there is something I want you to do for me, but mostly for the Lord. I want you to write a book about your journey with the Lord before it is too late. Will you do it?" That incident has now been past about twenty-five years. Finally, I am able to fulfill the pungent request of my friend. I said to him, "I am not a writer but maybe I will do it someday and get someone to make all the necessary corrections in it in order to make it readable. He said, "Don't let anybody get hold of it. If you do, they will ruin it. It will not be yours. A book does not have to be grammatically correct. Let it read like you said it."

With all of this said, this book will not be perfect but the fact is I am not perfect either. I have attempted to put into writing some of the things that God has done in my life. I do not want to call attention to myself but I want it to be to the glory and honor of my God and I want to give credit to all the wonderful people who have helped me along the way.

I would like to dedicate this book to my wife, Gladys, who has been my partner for sixty-five years and read my scribbled words and helped me to correct it. I would like to pay tribute to Sharon Kephart, who has typed and done the word processing and developing of this work. I would like to thank Karen Twiss for proof reading this book, Jack Lovin for writing "About the Author," and Dan Lunsford for writing the "Foreword."

Now, may God bless each person who reads any portion of this work. If someone reads it that is not a Christian, I admonish you to trust Jesus to save you. Tell Him you are a sinner and ask Him to come into your heart and then thank Him for saving you.

For all those who are my fellow Christians, I will see you in heaven some sweet day. "Well glory!"

I have failed much of the time and come very short in what I should have been, but God is always faithful. It is my goal to try to hold up the matchless goodness and loving grace of my Heavenly Father and His Son, Jesus Christ.

Starting Out on the Journey

The Beginnings of my Journey

God knows about every person who is born into this world and He has a definite plan for his or her life. March 7, 1925, a baby boy was born to Pearlie M. and Inez Rogers Lunsford in a little, obscure, mountain, community. They lived on the headwaters of Vengeance Creek in Cherokee County, N. C. There was some misunderstanding about this baby. When he got to be a teenager, he had an opportunity to get a job while in high school making three dollars per week, but he had to have a birth certificate. He was instructed to go to the County Register of Deeds Office to secure such a very important document. On searching the records, the Register of Deeds discovered that on March 7, 1925, a baby girl was born to Pearlie and Inez Lunsford. This was quite an embarrassing situation for him but he lived through it all and the records were changed and the name was put on the record as Fred Bruner Lunsford. The Doctor who delivered me was Dr. Fred Herbert. So I was named after him and then the "Bruner" part was my dad's idea after an old mountain horse-trader named "Bruner."

My paternal grandmother was Octavia O'Dell Lunsford, commonly called "Shug." She lived with my dad and mom. My grandmother said, "Poor child, I wouldn't name a dog that!" I will call him "Cooter" after old Uncle Cooter Lovingood on Hanging Dog. The nickname stuck. My family called me "Cooter" and today the name is still used by many. I never remember seeing this grandmother. I was born in March, and she died in October of the same year. Later, my maternal grandmother came to live with us. Her name was Ellen King Rogers. Most people called her Ella. I will mention her along the way, because she influenced my life greatly. She was born in the North Georgia Mountains. All of her children were born in Georgia. Her husband, my grandfather, was half Cherokee

3

Indian. They moved to Vengeance Creek at Marble, N. C. to live on tribal land when my mother was just a little girl. My grandmother never had the benefit of school, so she couldn't read or write but she memorized old hymns and some Bible verses. She trotted me on her knees and sang old songs to me such as "Amazing Grace, What a Friend we Have in Jesus, The Great Physician, and When I can Read my Title Clear to Mansions in the Sky." She would tell me stories of David and Goliath, Samson, Joseph, and Shamgar, who swapped ends of an ox goad and busted the heads of the Philistines.

My dad was a hard workingman, but not a Christian. My mother was one of the first people to be baptized into Vengeance Creek Baptist Church, which was organized in 1920. A man by the name of Grady King was staying with us working on the farm for his room and board. I was just about fifteen months old. The task at hand this time of year was cultivating the corn crop, which was vital to our survival. My dad and Grady plowed and hoed corn in the morning while my mother washed the breakfast dishes, took care of the milk from the cow, and cooked the noon meal that we called "dinner." The men came from the field and ate a dinner containing vegetables, pork, and milk. My mother cleaned up the dishes and got her hoe. With me in her arms, she would go to the cornfield to help hoe. In the afternoon, she spread a quilt down on the ground in the shade of an apple tree at the end of the field and then she sat me on it. She would hoe a short distance and keep an eye on me. Grady plowed out to the end, stopped the mule, and went to check on me. He discovered a large yellow rattlesnake crawling toward me at the edge of the quilt. I was waving my hands at the snake. My friend and protector ran as fast as he could and grabbed me as he jumped across the poisonous viper. The snake struck at him as he went over it, but just missed his leg. This mountain man rescued me from certain death. Grady's name never got in the paper, and he was never able to read or sign his name, but he has shared in the many things God has blessed me to accomplish for Him. As I share some of the things, remember, if it hadn't been for Grady, they never could have been. I shared this story in my former book, <u>Golden Nuggets from the Mountains</u>, but there is something important about it that I had forgotten. It recently came to my memory. My mother told me that she asked Grady why he went to check on me and he used his own grammar to tell her. He said, "God fer told me to." God used Grady to rescue me from sudden death. God has blessed me to see hundreds of souls saved in my lifetime. Grady will have a reward in heaven for all this because he obeyed God.

Life on the little mountain farm during the late 1920's and early 1930's was hard. We didn't know it was hard because everybody was in the same boat. We had no electricity and there was no running water in the house. We carried our water from the spring, which was some distance from the house, and we used kerosene lamps for light. During the depression days or "hard times" as some people called it, if a man could get a job for the going rate of one dollar per day or ten cents per hour for ten hours, they were glad for it. However, I never had to stand in line to get a bowl of soup and I never went hungry. We grew what we ate on the little farm. We had plenty of beans, potatoes, and corn. We always killed hogs in November or December, so we had pork and some wild meat along the way. God was good to us.

I always looked forward to going to Sunday School every Sunday at the old one-room schoolhouse in the community. The pastor came and preached one weekend each month. He preached on Saturday at 11:00 and conducted the church business meeting, which was called, "Monthly Conference." Sometimes, some very interesting business came up that was very entertaining to an inquisitive boy. On occasions, I remember when one of the church members would bring a charge against their fellow member for using bad language, going to parties, playing cards, drinking booze, dancing, and the list goes on. If the person confessed to the wrong they had done and asked forgiveness, they were pardoned and life went on as usual. If they didn't confess to the wrong and ask for forgiveness, then the church would vote to withdraw fellowship with them or "turn them out of the church" as it was often referred to. This practice has long since been abandoned. People don't like accountability anymore when it comes to religion. I learned some valuable lessons from these experiences. One of the things I learned was that one should never speak in anger because someone may be listening and especially because God listens. I also learned that if anything is questionable, don't do it.

Revival meetings were held once each year and most of the time it was in the month of August. The meetings went for two weeks and sometimes longer. Day services were held each and every day at 11:00 a.m. and the night service was held at 7:00 p.m. The pastor, along with one other preacher and maybe more, would stay with the people in the community. They would eat with different families. It was not unusual to hear people praying in the woods during the day. The men would quit work, put the horses in the barn, and go to church wearing their overalls for the 11:00 o'clock services. This was a big community event. Most everyone in the community went to the revival including both sinners and saints. At the close of the revival, they would dam the creek up and have a big baptizing on Sunday afternoon. Most of the time there were from ten to twenty-five new converts who were baptized. Church was a great part of my life when I was growing up and still is.

Those dedicated Christian men and women molded my life. We children would often play church, and most of the time I was the preacher. More than once, when a dog or cat would die, my sister would sing and I would preach the funeral and then we would put flowers on the new-made grave.

My Childhood and School Days

Dreaming, Learning, and the Big Challenge

As a child, I had many dreams for my life. Therefore, I grasped every learning opportunity, but there were always challenges before me. Daily, things were happening that gave me the opportunity to learn something new. I remember the very first time my dad took me with him to the blacksmith shop. He had a plow that needed to be sharpened, so he took me along with him. The shop was a dark, drab-looking place. Pieces of metal were scattered all over the place. A furnace built out of rock was near the corner. The old blacksmith took the small plow from my dad, stirred some ashes in the rock furnace, then he reached up, and began to pull a handle overhead. He pumped it up and down. I heard a blowing noise, and then I noticed the embers in the furnace begin to smoke, then a small flame came, and he laid some small pieces of coal on them. Now a fire was going as he kept pumping the air into it. Next, the metal plow was placed in the fire with some tongs that were lying nearby. After a little while, he took the plow out with the tongs and placed it on the anvil; it was red-hot. He began to hammer it. He was able to shape it the way he wanted it to be. He then placed it in a container filled with water. It fried and steamed as it cooled off. Now the plow was ready to be used for tilling the soil. This process really fascinated me.

I had a lot of questions as to why this or that but I learned a lesson that day that has stayed with me through the years. In Romans 12:2, it says, "And be not conformed to this world: but be ye transformed by the renewing of your mind, that ye may prove what is that good, and acceptable, and perfect, will of God." God is always seeking to mold and

9

fashion us after His will that we may be usable in His Kingdom. The Holy Spirit blows upon our hearts, fanning the flames of God's Word in us that we may be pliable enough to be molded after His will and purpose, rather than being molded by the world. "Well glory!"

From the very beginning of my life, God has in so very many ways, over and over again, sought to transform my life into something usable in His Kingdom. Many times, I have failed to yield to His making and He has had to put me through the fire to make me yield to His shaping.

A Devoted Companion

The days of growing up on the little mountain farm resulted in a life of surprises, never knowing what would be next. Of course, life any place is full of wonders.

Animals, both wild and domestic, played a big part in the life of those of us who were fortunate enough to grow up in such a blessed setting.

We had cows, mules, hogs, chickens, guineas, dogs, and cats. Then at various times, we encountered many wild animals. We depended a lot on animals for a part of our livelihood. We ate rabbits, squirrels, groundhogs, quail, grouse, deer, bear, and an opossum now and then.

From the domestic animals, we had milk from the cows, eggs from the chickens, pork from the hogs, and wool from the sheep. I heard an allegory once that went as follows: The chicken and the hog were having a conversation one day. The chicken said to the hog, "We are honored to provide breakfast for our masters' family. Do you not consider it a great honor to do this for this lovely family?" The hog said, "You can crow about this, but you only make a contribution while I have to make a bodily sacrifice."

One day there were some men up in the mountains above our house hunting. They encountered some wild mountain goats and killed one. It turned out that the one they killed was a mama goat that had a little kid goat. They brought it down to our house and dad put it in the corncrib. He and the hunters were discussing what to do with the little goat. Its mama was dead. I peeped through a crack of the crib and saw it lying in there all curled up, it was so cute. It looked at me with those pleading eyes and I fell in love with it. I began begging my dad to let me keep it. He said, "No, it will be too much trouble. It will starve to death. It can't eat. It is far too young. It must have milk to survive." I said, "I will fix it a bottle and give it some cows' milk. Please let me keep it." He then said, "Okay, but you will have the total responsibility of caring for it." I was ready to do anything to make it possible to keep the little creature. I had me a constant companion. Everywhere I went, so did the goat. I got in a lot of trouble because of that creature. It soon was eating anything and everything and that was a huge problem. One day, it followed me into the house. Mama came in the kitchen and I heard the commotion. The goat was standing on the table eating ham out of the meat dish. The goat got by lightly, but I caught the storm.

One day, my dad told me to tie the goat up with a chain and let it graze, so I tied it to an apple tree. That's where I made my big mistake. That unpredictable animal ate the bark off of the apple tree all the way around up as high as she could reach. It surely had a tremendous appetite for apple tree bark.

My dad saw what it had done and he said with a resounding voice, "I didn't tell you to tie it to my apple tree. Now the tree will die." Of course it did. I rode the goat, I played with the goat, but I never was able to make a Baptist out of it. My sister, my cousin, and I decided we would baptize that sinful creature. We dammed up the branch and created a pool of water that was deep enough to put her under. We dragged her into the water after a lot of effort. Once we were in the water, we started trying to put her head under the water and it would not go. We all got wet all over, except for the goat. Its head would not go under the water. My friend said, "This stubborn creature is a bad, bad, sinner. We sure don't want her to go to hell. I tell you what we will do. We will sprinkle her and make a Methodist out of her. Maybe that will do." I said, "It will have to do because it is too much for us." So, we ended up with a Methodist goat. That didn't change its devotion to me. It was still the same. Wherever I went, there was the goat.

It surely must have been a trauma for me when I had to part with a devoted animal, but for the life of me; I cannot remember what ever happened to that goat. I have heard it said that sometimes when one has a horrible experience in life, he would shut it out of his mind. That could have happened to me or God could have erased it from my memory for my benefit. All I know is I don't remember what ever happened to it.

The Era of the Rolling Store

During the decade of the 1930's, mountain people did the best they could with what they had. They grew most of their food by tilling the loamy, mountain soil. They cured their meat, made molasses, and pickled, dried, and canned vegetables. We had apple trees, so my mom dried apples, and preserved them any way she could. My dad would dig a hole in the base of a haystack and put Limber Twig and Wine Sap Apples in it and cover them with hay so we could have fresh apples to eat most of the winter. Although we grew most of our food, there were some basic necessities that we had to buy.

The closest grocery store from our house was at Marble, about four miles away. We had no car; very few people did. Now and then, my dad would take the wagon to town and would buy some necessary things, but not very often. Therefore, it was necessary to walk the four miles when we needed something.

A new day dawned and the rolling store came into being. On certain days the big truck with the bed all boxed in with shelves and bins would make its appearance down the road. I would go with my mother to meet it. This was a big event. She would save eggs from the chickens and use them for cash. Now and then, we would catch an old hen or two and tie their legs together and carry them down the road. We waited for the store truck in the shade of a big tree by the side of the road.

Every vehicle that we heard, we thought that surely this was it. I had my eyes fastened on the curve in the road a few yards away listening for the truck. When it would turn out to be a log truck or a pulp wood truck, I was disappointed, but, finally, there it came around the curve with a chicken coop tied on the front bumper with several chickens and sometimes ducks in it. On the back was a large tank that contained kerosene oil. Everybody had to have kerosene. Sometimes, it was called lamp oil for kerosene lamps and lanterns. We had no electricity. The man who ran this rolling store was a man by the name of Ed Graves. He also had a general store on Hanging Dog. It was in the Ebenezer section of Hanging Dog Community. Ebenezer Baptist Church was also close by Ed's store.

It was most interesting to observe the women of the community as they shopped at the rolling super market. It was stocked with most any and everything that you might need. My mother bought her a new straw hat to wear in the garden. It cost twenty cents. One of the absolute necessities was snuff. Most of the women dipped snuff, and if they were out of snuff, they were all out of sorts. They would argue as to which brand was the best. Some said Garrett's was the best while others said Bruton's was better. Now and then I would get a piece of candy and what a treat this was for me.

As far as I know, Ed Graves started the store truck business and then later on Gene Fair had one and Frank Kephart. Frank ran the store truck for many years. He went to my dad's house on the head of Vengeance Creek. Dad bought everything from cow feed to Epson's Salts from him. Frank also had a general store in Hanging Dog Community. He was a highly respected businessman as well as a Deacon of Ebenezer Baptist Church. He was a noted singer. He raised a fine family of seven children along with his devoted wife, Josephine. Two of their children who were twins have been, now for many years, a great help to me in the ministry. Karen was my Administrative Assistant while I was Director of Missions for twelve years and is still serving the Lord in that position. Sharon is Secretary/Treasurer of my Christian Lighthouse Ministry, Inc. and does all the work of putting my books together. Frank and Josephine's other children are all devoted Christian workers.

The store truck, as well as the country store, has long since been replaced by the supermarkets and convenience stores, but not without making a large contribution to the well being of many people. All those I knew left behind a good and lasting witness for the Lord, Jesus Christ. By their very nature, a devoted Christian flows forth a positive witness for the Gospel of Jesus Christ. Acts 1:8 says, "But ye shall receive power, after that the Holy Ghost is come upon you: and ye shall be witnesses unto me both in Jerusalem, and in all Judea, and in Samaria, and unto the uttermost part of the earth." Thank God for godly mountain families that literally blanket the land with the Gospel of Jesus Christ.

The Glory of the Mountaintop

"I will lift up mine eyes unto the hills, from whence cometh my help." Psalms 121:1. The author of this verse was an exile on the plains of Babylonia. He no doubt was held a captive far away from the hills and mountains of his native home. Many times I have served in the plains and in the busy cities of our country. I always find myself longing for the hills of home. I am sure the soul of the writer of Psalms 121 was free, although his body was in bondage. The hills of his fatherland were not far away from the eye of his spirit. Strength of soul and power of spirit came to him from the upward look. The hills remained the source of his power and support of his faith and courage. He received spiritual help from the very memory of the hills; his eyes were fastened on the horizon toward the unseen heights beyond.

I grew up in the shadow of a mountain in Western North Carolina called the "Peachtree Bald." This towering mountain was always a challenge and inspiration to me. Many times I have stood and watched the Eastern sun peep up over this lovely, graceful, and rugged mountain. There is nothing like the beauty of this enchanting sunrise. How about standing with me and viewing the big orange moon just edging up over the mountain. I longed for the day when I could climb that mountain. These lines are somewhat about my journey as God has privileged me to climb the mountain of life. "I will lift mine eyes unto the hills, from whence cometh my help."

Dwellers among the hills and mountains have always felt the inspiring and elevating influence of the heights in which they live. We are molded by our physical environment, as well as by our moral and spiritual environment. Mountain folk have always been men of rugged and sturdy nature, honest, industrious, and religious. It was among the hills of Scotland that there was developed a unique national religious life and spirit. It was also among the hills of New England and along the coast that our own nation was cradled in liberty, righteousness, and justice. It was in the hill-country of Galilee and Judea that the Master of Life lived and loved and labored. When cares weighed heavy upon His soul, He sought the invigorating welcome of the hillside and mountain, where there was breathed into His heart a message of courage and hope.

The hills and heights are constantly voicing spiritual messages. We hear the mountains and uplands among which we live and move. We live in a land that is rich in its beauty of hills and mountains. Nature seems to have lavished the wealth of her charm and glory around us on every side. If we listen, we can hear the messages that pour in from every nook, corner, valley, and mountain...messages of power, and of spiritual help. They are messages from God, the God who made and owns the hills and mountains, as well as the trees, the rivers, and every object of His creation. "The strength of the hills is His also." The language of the hills is interpreted not so much by the reason as by the higher emotions, and by the deeper impulses of the heart and soul. When we attempt to translate the message of the hills, our thoughts will roam from path to path, from peak to peak, striving to put together bits and pieces of the scene that might be viewed as the whole, catching notes of the melody now and then which imagination must blend into harmony and tune. As wooded groves were probably the first temples where the early worshippers lifted their hearts to God, no doubt altars were erected here and there. I well remember an old mountain preacher that frequented a special place of prayer on the mountain. Each visit he made to this special place, he carried with him a stone. There remains to this day a large pile of stones with each stone representing a time that this rugged man of God visited with his God in private worship. A consciousness of the Divine Presence invested the hills with mystery and awe and reverence. The eye that looks downward sees the valley and gulches and ravines, but the eyes that pierce upward behold the sanctuaries of God. Jesus often sought the quiet of the hilltop to drink in faith and hope and power. His greatest sermon was delivered not in a church, but on the mount. It was on the Mount of Transfiguration that His glory was revealed to the three disciples, and it was on the green hill outside the city wall where He breathed His last breath as a mortal. His life was in constant companionship with the hills and heights because His life was the life of all mountaintop life. Life may be lived on any level, on the plain, or on the heights, but the level on which we live determines our character and destiny. Jesus never descended to the environment of His day, but endeavored to lift the environment to the level where He was living. His life brought heaven to earth, and raised earth nearer to heaven. Even so, as we ascend the peaks of the spiritual life, we do not rid ourselves entirely of the valleys, but as we ascend, we carry the valleys with us and find that if we are filled with the Spirit "every valley shall be exalted." While Israel was on the desert plains, the people were but wandering nomads, but when they entered the hill-country of Canaan, they became a nation. They became great only when they left the level lands and became mountain folk in the hills and highlands of Palestine. Living in the highlands of the soul attains spiritual greatness, like national greatness.

The mountains are a source of aspiration. When a mountain looms before us, we cannot look down, but the sight draws our eyes upward. When I go to the flatland for a few days to preach a revival or do a conference, I have a good time. What a joy it is to serve the Lord anywhere, anytime; however, when I head back to my home in the hills, I look straight ahead looking for the first hill or mountain. As tourists cross the plains, they never look back but are charmed by the majesty and attractive power of heights that are before them. The hills invite us to rise above the trivial and commonplace, nearer to the home of God. We lift up our eyes unto the hills and find that there is an infinite reservoir of strength in the upward look.

The hill challenges our strength, courage, and perseverance. The tramp is seldom a hill climber, but a drifter, a plodder of the plains and level stretches. The up-roads of the lands of the spirit are traveled not by wanderers, drifters, and the lazy, but by sturdy seekers after God. "Then said Jesus unto his disciples, If any man will come after me, let him deny himself, and take up his cross, and follow me." Matthew 16:24. The hills have little attraction for the idler, but are filled with charm for the pilgrim who aspires higher ground.

The hills are the source of life-giving streams. Back in the mountain, we find the springs that replenish the brooks, creeks, and rivers. In some unsuspected place within the hills, we discover the source of the great rivers that carry life to the level-lands and valleys. Even so, when we explore the mountain peaks of the spiritual life, we discover the source of the streams of grace and joy and love, which bring life to the lower arid levels of life. From every mountaintop of the soul, there shall flow streams of life-giving Spiritual water.

We are living in two worlds. We are living in a world of sense, a world that we see, a world of trees, hills, streams, and rivers, friend, and all the objects that lift the senses and enrich our earthly lives. This world is not to be despised or denounced, but to be enjoyed to the fullest. We are also citizens of another world of the Spirit.

The eye of the soul can see that the landscapes of this Spiritual realm outshines the physical realms like a thousand chandeliers would outshine one little flickering candle or as the Niagara Falls would overshadow a little mud puddle after a spring rain. There are highlands as well as lowlands in the land of the Spirit. Mountain peaks and valleys meet us at every turn of the road. As we rise above the lower levels to the mountain summits of the soul, we find that the reward awaiting us at the journey's end will be the satisfaction of having reached the summit with it's clear atmosphere, it's broader vision, and it's seclusion from the ills, strains, and scars of the lowlands. As we reach the life that is nearer to God, we discover that the greatest reward for our effort and toil is the satisfaction that comes from having left behind the sordid, drab, commonplace and dull, and having become a citizen of a loftier, higher, land. This is the land of the expanding horizon, the land of the broad and tolerant vision; the land that sees first the rising light of God and follows the sun at last to it's setting in the West. The hilltop life in the world of the Spirit is the life that is lived nearest to God. "I will lift up mine eyes unto the hills from whence cometh my help."

Growing up in the shadow of the great majestic Peachtree Mountain, I dreamed of the day that I could climb this rugged mountain. What a challenge and aspiration. The day finally came that my dad said I could go. My mother packed us some lunch to take along. The task was to take some salt to our cattle that were on the mountain for the summer. As we traveled along, I kept my eyes on the mountain, but kept remembering the cornbread and fried country ham, along with the fried apple pies and big red June apples in the sack tied on my dads' back. We could eat at the top of the mountain. A thirsty boy drank from a cool, sparkling, spring bubbling from a solid rock at the base of the mountain. The sun was hot and the mountain steep, but the goal was the top. Then finally, the top was in sight. Now we sat on a big tree that had fallen right on top. The cars on U. S. Highway 19 going from Murphy to Andrews in the valley looked like small insects crawling along. A cool breeze was blowing upon my brow as I brushed away puddles of perspiration. Wild flowers were blooming and the birds were singing. Spontaneously, words came from my lips, "Can we eat?" Now we enjoyed a banquet sitting on a log on the summit of Peachtree Bald. When I returned home, I could tell the story of what was on the other side of the mountain.

Now, having lived almost eighty-four years and having been in the ministry almost sixty years, I have climbed many spiritual mountains and am still on the journey. God has promised us power for the journey. He has also promised us that He will go with us all the way.

The marvelous parallel stands before us. As we climb these spiritual mountains with God, when we reach the top, we too can sit down with Him to enjoy the glory and beauty. "Well glory!"

School Days

I started school in a little one-room schoolhouse, which was for grades one through seven. Vengeance Creek schoolhouse was used as a meeting place for Vengeance Creek Baptist Church as well as for school. School had been going two weeks when they consolidated Vengeance Creek School with Marble School about three miles away. The first school bus was a pulp wood truck boxed in like a cattle truck. My dad wouldn't let me ride that kind of "outfit" as he called it. So I didn't get to go to school the first year, but I had a book. During that year, I dreamed of going to school. While I was dreaming, I learned the alphabet as well as how to spell simple words. When I started to school the next year, I soon was promoted to the second grade. My teacher was Miss Kate Hayes, a great Christian lady. She read the Bible and had prayer each morning. She insisted that all of her students memorize Psalm 23. That has meant much to me all through the years. I have quoted it to myself in foxholes when the battle was raging, and the times when life was as dark as midnight. This Scripture gave me strength in knowing that the Lord was indeed my Shepherd. "Well glory!"

There were times that I had to miss school to help out due to sickness or to help on the farm. However, my teachers were people with a lot of devotion to their pupils, so I never failed a grade. They were very helpful.

I graduated from Andrews High School in May of 1943 and went into the Army in August. Army days are another story.

There were many interesting episodes in my childhood days that contributed greatly to my education. During these school days, I had a very sick spell. I think I was in the third grade. I had a high fever; my head hurt, and I ached all over. All the home remedies were used with no avail. My dad walked four miles to Marble and got Dr. Smart to come see me. House calls were the norm for doctors in those days. He checked me over, looked at my tongue, looked in my ears, eyes, and throat, felt of my neck, my back, and my belly. He asked to go see our water bucket. We didn't have electricity. We carried our water from the spring. The bucket our water was in was a wooden bucket. He came back and asked me some questions. One question was the key to the whole problem. He said, "What kind of water bucket do they have at the school?" I knew quite well about the water system. It was a very common system of the day. The children carried water in a zinc water bucket from a nearby spring. Each room had a bucket and a dipper. Then he said, "Have you been drinking that water?" Of course, the answer was "Yes." He then asked, "Do you ever remember drinking early in the morning?" I thought awhile and I usually did get a drink when I first got to school. The water had been sitting in the bucket over night or perhaps over the weekend. He said, "You have zinc poisoning. " He gave me some pills to kill the poison and went to the schoolhouse and examined the water buckets. He found that they were beginning to rust. He made them get rid of all the buckets and replaced them with non-zinc ones. Of course I recovered rapidly and was soon back in school drinking from the new white water bucket.

The most life-changing event during my school days occurred when I was thirteen years old. I was saved in August of 1938. Of course, this was the greatest thing that ever happened to me. Salvation is not only for this life but also for eternity. That same year, something else happened that has been very important to me through the years. The Tennessee Valley Authority started building dams on the rivers to produce electricity. This was a big move for the area. Power would be available for all people in the mountains. Of course, for this to happen they had to employ people to build the dams. My dad got a job helping clear the right-of-way for Hiawassee Dam and later, Chatuge Dam at Hayesville, N. C. He started out making forty-seven and one half cents per hour. That surely did beat ten cents an hour or fifteen cents at the most all during the 1930's.

TVA, of course, bought up all the land in the Hiawassee River Basin that was covered with water. The families had to find a home wherever they could. Some families moved to our community.

One morning I got on the school bus. It was just a common, ordinary morning. Everybody was talking and giggling as usual. Then the school bus stopped and a little short girl got on the bus and sat down right near me. She was the most beautiful girl I had ever seen. She was just eleven years old, two years younger than I was. She had a toboggan on, knee socks, and saddle oxfords as well as other clothes, but I don't remember what they looked like. She looked at me and smiled. I asked what her name was and she said, "Gladys Greene." I said, "Oh yes, I know now you are part of the Greene family that moved in from Hiawassee River, West of Murphy, N. C." From then on, she became an outstanding person to me. When she was seventeen and I was nineteen, I was in the Army. After basic training, I came home on leave before going overseas. We went to Blairsville, GA and she became my wife. She now has been a faithful and dedicated hard working companion for almost sixty-five years. She is the mother of my two boys and the grandmother of my grandchildren.

I had many wonderful classmates in high school as well as some very good dedicated teachers. I pay tribute to all of them. Many of them have already departed this life. When I think of those people who have made an everlasting contribution to my life, I remember teachers like Miss Kate Hayes, Rev. Paul Lovingood, Miss Jean Christy, Mrs. Aline Bristol, and Mr. Guy Sutton, as well as many others. I remember a multitude of fellow students like Ray Hogsed, John Clark, Doris McConnell, Buck McConnell, Lucy Long, Faye Buchanan, Julia Brown, Lenora Mosteller, and many others. Neither time nor space will allow me to name them all. They are all very important to me. I thank God for every one of them.

Most experiences in life's journey have spiritual applications if we look for them. When they happened, I never thought of spiritual or life applications, but as I look back on them, I realize all the while, God was speaking to me through them.

In my days of growing up, we didn't have a lot of structured activities for young people, so we had to create our own entertainment. Out of these activities, a lot of very important lessons were learned.

Drinking From the Rock

One Sunday afternoon, some of us boys were out in the green fields and shady lanes of the beautiful enchanted hills playing, running, climbing trees, and wading the cool, trickling, fresh, mountain streams. We came to one such stream and waded it. The mountain water felt so cool to my feet. I was hot and thirsty as a result of running and playing in the hot summer sun. I decided I would get me a drink of that cool, mountain water. Everybody doesn't know that we all have a built in pump to get water when needed, but I knew this quite well. I had used this equipment many times. So I knelt down and put my mouth in a pool of the little brook and began to drink, but as I did, the other boys began to laugh. I wondered why they were laughing. When my thirst was completely quenched, I asked them why they were laughing, but they continued to laugh at me, and then pointed in the ripples of the brook just two or three feet above where I was drinking to a dead snake lodged on a rock. I was so controlled by my thirst, that I failed to see the contamination caused by the dead snake. The lesson learned here is that I could have gone up stream about one hundred feet to the spring bubbling out of a solid rock. It would have been pure as pure could be.

The spiritual application here is that we are proned to listen to what people of this world say and be influenced and controlled thereby. We shouldn't do this since we have the opportunity to go and receive from the Solid Rock, Jesus Christ. "And did all drink the same spiritual drink: for they drank of that spiritual Rock that followed them: and that Rock was Christ."-I Corinthians 10:4.

Holidays at our House

The only holidays that were very significant were Christmas, Easter and, of course, Memorial Day. The Fourth of July and Labor Day were just another day, perhaps mentioned in passing. Most of the time, Christmas was not the best for me, to say the least. Instead of the abundance of gifts that children receive today, an orange, a stick of hard peppermint candy, and sometimes, one small gift, like a little rubber ball, was what we got. We would peel the orange and lay the peeling up and let it dry and eat it later, a small piece at a time. I dreaded Christmas, because for some reason, some of the men in the community would get drunk on moonshine, including my dad. This was a horrible experience for me. They would curse, fight, and abuse their wives and children. I would hide by crawling under the bed. Due to all of this, the celebrating of our blessed Saviour's birth was a sad time for me. Of course, my mother would bake a cake if she had the materials to use. She usually did because she would save some flour, eggs, sugar and chocolate for this purpose. On one Christmas that I remember very well, my dad was not drunk and we went hunting in the snow on Christmas morning and we killed some rabbits and a squirrel for Christmas dinner.

Memorial Day was called Decoration Day when everybody went to the cemetery and put flowers on the graves of their loved ones. It was a very solemn time and yet it was a time the people got together for a time of fellowship. They would bring their song books and sing a few old Gospel songs. The preacher would preach, or if the preacher was not available, a layman would talk and perhaps, some would talk about the loved ones who had gone on to heaven. These events made an impression for good on the mind of an impressionable child and the memories linger with me in my old age.

Easter was the best of all. No gifts were expected and nobody got drunk. Spring had come, the long hard winter had passed, the flowers were blooming, and the birds were singing. On Good Friday, the Friday before Easter, we planted beans in the garden. Come Easter Sunday morning, we had all the fried eggs we wanted, but other times, they were rationed because we used eggs for cash at the rolling store. We also had plenty of boiled eggs dyed various colors, using different herbs for die such as indigold, blood root, and polk berries. Church was on Easter Sunday and it was a time when everybody wore the best they had. They gathered together to celebrate the resurrection of Jesus Christ. One thing that always bothered me was on the Friday before Easter when Jesus was crucified, a period of total darkness ocurred at mid-day as Jesus was hanging on the cross, but God, in time, revealed to me as to why this occurred. So in the next section, I will share what God has shown me that has brought me a lot of peace and reconciliation about this event.

THE DARKNESS OF THE DARKEST HOURS

Matthew 27:45:-"Now from the sixth hour there was darkness over all the land unto the ninth hour." No darkness has ever been as dark as these three hours.

People were gazing at Him hanging there on the cross. Matthew 27:36 says, "And sitting down they watched Him there." They were mocking Him, making all kinds of sport of Him as if it was an event of entertainment. The religious leaders mocked Him. Matthew 27:41: "Likewise also the chief priest mocking Him, with the scribes and elders." Then something happened unexpected at the sixth hour, 12:00 noon. Total darkness covered the land. I can visualize people scrambling, bumping into each other falling over objects trying to find a torch to light. There were no electric lights, and no flashlights. What a time of confusion!

They no longer could see Him on the cross. They could not look at each other and laugh. The laughing turned into crying. All the merry making was silenced. This darkness has great spiritual significance. Some have said that it was an eclipse of the sun. That is impossible, because the Passover was always on the full moon. It has been described as natures' sympathy with the suffering Lord, but that is a pagan conception of nature. Some say it was an act of God because of His sympathy with His Son. This is to deny the cry of Jesus that followed the darkness. Matthew 27:46: "And about the ninth hour Jesus cried with a loud voice, saying, E-li, E-li, la-masa-bach-tha-ni? That is to say, My God, My God, why hast thou forsaken me?"

The big question is why the darkness and where did it come from?

What was this darkness? What did it really mean?

In Luke 22:53 Jesus says to those who came to arrest Him, "When I was daily with you in the temple, ye stretched forth no hands against me: but this is your hour, and the power of darkness." We will ponder this very suggestive word very carefully. At the beginning of our Lord's ministry, He referred to an hour, which was not yet. One of the profoundest sayings of Jesus illuminating His own ministry was, "I must work the works of Him that sent me, while it is day: the night cometh, when no man can work."- John 9:4: That was the consummating hour to which He looked; the time of darkness that at last would come in which no man could work, but God alone must work.

At Gethsemane, the soldiers were about to lay hands on Him and lead Him away to Caiaphas, to Pilate, to Herod, and again to Pilate, and to death. Before they did, He said, "This is your hour and the power of darkness." The hour had arrived and its character was that of darkness. John says in his first epistle in I John 1:5, "This then is the message which we have heard of Him and declare unto you, that God is light and in Him is no darkness at all."

From the sixth hour to the ninth hour, there was darkness in all the land. It was a period of infinite silence; a period of overwhelming darkness.

In these three hours, we see the Savior in the midst of all that which resulted from the action of evil. The apostle Paul spoke in a letter to Ephesus of Satan as the "Prince of the Power of the Air." He spoke of him as being ruler of the darkness. Satan's supreme desire was and is to extinguish the Light, but Jesus is the Light and Jesus is Eternal.

From the very beginning of the shining of that Light focused in history by the incarnation, the one supreme purpose of the enemy was to apprehend it, to comprehend it, to extinguish it, to put it out. In these three hours of darkness, we are brought face to face with the time when all the forces of evil were brought to bear on the soul of the Son of God. All the unutterable intent and purpose of evil wrapped Him in a darkness that is beyond our comprehension. He experienced the total darkness of sin and evil that we might have and be the Light of the World.

This time of physical darkness is a symbol of the empire of sin. Take a look at the following statements, and we will immediately see how that darkness is a symbol of spiritual evil. "The people which sat in darkness"- Matthew 4:16. "If thine eye be evil thy whole body shall be full of darkness.

If therefore the light that is in thee be darkness, how great is the darkness," Matthew 6:23. "The sons of the kingdom shall be cast forth into the outer darkness," Matthew 8:12. "Cast ye out the unprofitable servant into the outer darkness," Matthew 25:30.

Darkness is the twin sister of death. Death and darkness express the ultimate of evil. The material darkness was but the outward and visible sign of the more mysterious and unfathomable spiritual darkness into the midst of which He had to pass through. The darkness was of Satan. When God, the Father, turned His back on His Son to die, Satan had his chance to send his darkness.

The Passing of the Darkness

That we may understand the passing of the darkness, let us look again at the four words that fell from the lips of the Lord just beyond the ninth hour when the darkness was passing away and the light of day was again breaking through the darkness to reveal the green hill and the cruelty of the cross. Notice the four cries that fell from His lips.

The first cry was the expression of a backward thought, "My God, My God, why has thou forsaken me?" It was a call from Jesus as He emerged from the darkness and all that happened therein. It was in itself a revelation like a flash of lightening, dispelling the darkness. The next word we hear is an expression of His conscious humanity, "I thirst."

Almost immediately following it, we have "It is finished." He who is Light has conquered darkness. The final word described is a forward look. As the first word beyond the darkness is a backward look, the last word is a forward look; a confidence in the Father's good will. "Father, into thy hands I commend my Spirit."

The death that saves is not that of physical dissolution, but the infinite spiritual mystery that occurred in the three hours of darkness. The battle was raging and "The Light" won over darkness forever. He, Himself, did say, "It is finished."

After the passing of darkness, Satan is not present. Loving hands took His body from the cross and carefully laid Him to rest. The Word says in Colossians 2:15, "And having spoiled principalities and powers, He made a show of them openly, triumphing over them in it." In the midst of the darkness, He gained victory over the forces of evil.

The aspect of that transaction is much larger than we can know in this life, but in God's own way, "The stone which the builder's had rejected is become the head of the corner." This is the Lord's doing, and it is marvelous in our eyes.- Matthew 21:42

We sing, "Love so Amazing, so Divine," and "Amazing Grace How Sweet the Sound." I cannot explain all that happened. All I know is that He passed through that ultimate darkness for me that I might not have to pass that way. I will pass into the marvelous light. They taunted Him by saying, "He saved others, He cannot save Himself." He would not save Himself in order to save me.

World War II Days

A Life Changing Event-Army Beginnings

I was a senior in high school looking toward graduation in the spring. We had been having some frosty mornings and a little snow now and then. I had a wonderful girl friend. Everything was really looking up for me. Communication was not much in those days since there were no televisions and very few people had a radio. Most of the news I got was in school. We were in class on December 8, 1942. The principal, Mr. Hudson, came to our room and interrupted the teacher to give us the tragic news. Japan had bombed Pearl Harbor the day before. The President declared war on Japan and everything changed. Some of the boys in our class who were already eighteen went away to war and didn't get to graduate. In the spring of 1943, I graduated from high school after turning eighteen in March. My first day after my birthday, I was to register for the draft. That summer, after the crops were planted, I went to the Snowbird Mountains to work on a logging job for a man named, Grant Phillips. Mr. Phillips was cutting large oak trees and transporting them to the sawmill with horses. He then sawed them into timbers, trucked them to Marble, and loaded them on freight cars. From there, they were shipped to a shipyard in Norfolk, Virginia to be used for shipbuilding. I slept in the bunkhouse and ate in the chow hall working ten hours a day. I don't remember how much money I made, but the going wage was ten cents per hour.

In the month of July, I received greetings from the President of the United States that I had been drafted into the military to help fight the war. I was to report to the bus station in Murphy early in the morning of August 12. Three busloads of young men (most were eighteen years old) were there. We were ready to fight for our Country. When I got my notice, Grant Phillps told me that his logging job was a defense job and he could get me a deferment for six months if I wanted him to do so. I said, "No, I will go on and do my duty for my Country." We went to Camp Croft, South Carolina for our examination and induction into service. Some of us went in the Navy, some in the Marines, and some in the Army. We came home for a few days and then went back to Fort Jackson, S. C.

The first night at Fort Jackson was a horrible night. I had never felt so alone in all of my life. It fell my lot to sleep on the second floor of the barracks and of all things, on the top bunk. It must have been one hundred and ten degrees on that top bunk right up against the roof where the hot South Carolina sun had been beaming down all day long. I was just laying there sweating and thinking about being home sitting on the front porch of the old farm house, feeling the cool mountain breeze blowing on my fevered brow. Then eleven o'clock came and they started playing taps. The loud speakers were just outside our window. I thought I would die. I thought surely the world had come to an end. I cried myself to sleep and dreamed of home. The next morning, we had to fall out for reveille at five o'clock and start the day running without slowing down all day long. We had to have another physical and one shot right after another. Then we had to endure another long, hot, lonely night. I was a Christian, but hadn't had a lot of practice praying, but those few days at Fort Jackson, I caught up on my praying, if there is such a thing as that. God heard and answered my feeble prayers. He manifested Himself to me in a mighty way and the Scripture that says "I will never leave you nor forsake you," came close to me. He was a constant companion to me all through the war and all through life. He never leaves me, even in old age.

Several of the young men were from Cherokee County and some I had gone to school with. I had hoped we would stay together, but it was not so. Donald Cook and myself had gone to school together and grew up in the same community. One morning, Don was gone. He had shipped out to some place and we didn't know where. John Clark, with whom I had graduated from high school, was still there, as well as Homer Hunsucker and Dan Hughes from Murphy. One night, they rounded a bunch of us up like cattle in a coral and loaded us on a troop train. We had no idea where we were headed. Late in the night, the train stopped. A man was walking along the track and I yelled out the window to him and asked where we were and he said, "Knoxville, TN." Daylight brought some big surprises. We were at the train depot in Louisville, KY. Our faces were all black from the coal smoke from the old steam locomotive. Our army-tan uniforms were all black as well. GI Trucks gave us immediate transportation to Fort

Knox, KY. We were now a part of the Armored Force of the U. S. Army, and ready for basic training. What a sad looking crew!

Basic Training at Fort Knox

Fort Knox, Kentucky is famous for more things than a place for storage of gold. During World War II, it was famous for producing tough soldiers. They were determined to make you or break you. It was the Army Center for training people for the Armored Force, mainly tank crews. It consisted of thirteen weeks of very intensive training, six weeks of infantry training, six weeks of tank training, and one week of battle training. The first six weeks were the worst. To begin with, they took us out to a field that was grown up with weeds, sprouts, and briars. They gave us a rifle and instructed us to crawl across the field in a cold rain and sleet. As I crawled through the mud and briars, I thought I would surely freeze to death. I prayed to my God for help to be able to endure. We finally came out on the other side. Some of the leaders were there with big containers of hot beef bouillon. I had never tasted any of the stuff before, but I thought the hot stuff was the best thing I had ever tasted. The hot liquid really warmed me up and I thanked God. The old mess Sergeant said, "You ought to thank me." I replied, "Well, I do thank you, but you are an answer to my prayers."

The first Sunday I was there, I went to the Battalion Chapel for church services. I believed then and still believe that a Christian ought to be totally committed to God and be faithful to His church. That first Sunday, the Chaplain really impressed me as a man of God. He preached a wonderful message and gave an invitation for total dedication to God. I went to the altar to pray along with several others. As I talked to the Chaplain, I discovered he was a Methodist. Of course, I was a Baptist, but that really didn't matter. Chaplain Fritz became a dear friend. I soon was serving as an usher and assistant to him. God really blessed by giving me the opportunity to serve in this way. I grew as a Christian and learned a lot that has been a help to me through the years. God is always good in whatever situation or place we find ourselves, but we must trust Him.

Many very interesting things happened in Basic Training. Long hikes, with a full field pack, occurred quite frequently. First, five miles, then ten miles, then fifteen, now twenty, and the big one was thirty miles. We always went up Agony Hill and then Misery Hill through mud holes and creeks.

We learned to march, keeping time with the Drill Sergeants' command and now and then, we had to march with the band. The Battalion Retreat Parade was a big event with dress uniforms. The M-1 Rifle was our primary weapon. We had to learn how to disassemble it and then put it back together. We had to do it so much that we could do it while blindfolded.

We learned to drive all the vehicles of the Army, from the jeep to the large tank. Some men knew how to drive, but I didn't because we never owned a car. I ended up being a qualified tank driver.

The last week of training was battle training, sleeping in tents out in the field in the month of January 1944. I was issued a tank with a full crew. I was the driver, had an assistant driver, a gunner, and a tank commander. My commander was a Second Lieutenant, just out of Officers Candidate School. He was twenty years old and had never been in a tank before. He had spent ninety days in Officers School. We called them "Ninety Day Wonders." I, a Private, was supposed to teach a commissioned officer everything about a tank in a battle environment. It was cold, rainy, and muddy. We went out one morning before daylight. We came to a creek that we had to drive through. I told the Lieutenant since he was the Tank Commander that he was supposed to dismount (that is to get out of the tank), and take his bayonet and probe the bottom of the creek for land mines before we crossed. He proceeded to do so. His weapon was a Forty-five Caliber Thompson Sub-Machine Gun, which was strapped on his shoulder. The strap came unbuckled, and the gun fell in the creek. He ran his arm down in the muddy water to his shoulder and retrieved his weapon, all covered with mud. I couldn't help but laugh. He was a good-natured young man and I am sure he did well. Before we parted company, I found out that he was a Christian. Battle Training was over and we were now all trained and ready for war. We came back to camp and cleaned everything up and got our orders. We had a ten-day leave on our way to Fort Mead, Maryland.

I got on the bus in Louisville, Kentucky and went from there to Nashville, Tennessee. I changed buses and headed to Chattanooga. I changed buses again and boarded the Trailway Bus and headed for Asheville, N. C. I got off at Marble, N. C., which was one hundred miles before Asheville. The eight days at home went by so fast. I got to see all my folks and my girl, Gladys, everyday. While I was at home, we got engaged to be married. I then caught a bus to Asheville, another to Salisbury, N. C., and then a train to Union Station in Washington, D. C. A bus was waiting to take us to Fort Mead. While at Fort Mead, we went to A. P. Hill, Virginia for maneuvers. I drove a tank the entire distance, crossing the Potomac River. While there, orders came through that I had a furlough. I could go home. I followed the same route home that I had followed going up there. It ended up that I had three nights at home. This is when the big event happened. When I found out that I had a short furlough, I wrote Gladys and told her that if she wanted to, we would get married while I was at home. The first night I was home, I spent most of the night at her house discussing the matter at hand, and talking about what the future held. On the morning of the seventeenth of March, we went to Blairsville, Georgia and got married by a man running a little print shop. He was what they called the Ordinary. I think he was like a Justice of the Peace in North Carolina. Now we were married, after all we were getting older. She had just turned seventeen on February 25, and I, much older, had turned nineteen on March 7. I was home with my bride two nights and then I had to leave to get back to Fort Mead by the deadline. It was sad parting, but I had to go trusting God as I went and looking forward to the day I would return.

To Europe

When I arrived at camp, I received word that we were scheduled to ship out overseas soon. So, the process started. There were more examinations and shots. Different clothing and equipment were issued. We boarded the ship on April 6, 1944 at Pier 51. A big snow had fallen the night before. We all had to be loaded before daybreak. We sailed out of New York early in the morning while the snow was still falling aboard the British Ship, Aquataina. It was the fourth largest ship in the world. It was hauling thirteen thousand troops plus the crew. It took us nine days across the Atlantic, zigzagging our course to dodge German submarines, arriving in Glasgow, Scotland and then boarding a train to Wells, England. There, we slept in a tent in a cow pasture. While in Wells, we had more intensive training. However, because I had typing in high school, they sent me to London to Clerical School, and I became a Clerk Typist. When we got back to Wells, we were now ready for the Normandy Invasion. I went in on Omaha Beach, two or three days after the first wave of troops that stormed the beach. Some of my buddies were in that first wave and many of them were killed. We anchored ship out in the English Channel, and climbed down a rope ladder into a landing craft that took us to the shore. The front of the boat let down on the Beach, and we ran ashore through water about knee-deep. We ran toward a steep incline that rose quickly from the beach under enemy fire, coming from bunkers on the hill ahead. An enemy bullet hit my best friend as we climbed up the incline, but we had to go on and leave him there to die.

A short distance from the beach, we pitched our tents and dug in for a few days. Bulldozers were brought ashore. They dug a large channel and rolled the bodies of our comrades in the hole and covered them up. This is now the famous Cemetery of Normandy, with all the white crosses representing those who are buried there.

We were now in General Patton's Third Army, moving across France with a tremendous, aggressive, force and headed toward Germany. Many things happened that I could write about. It would take volumes to contain the happenings, but I will touch on a few highlights that I feel are very important. These things helped mold my life for the future.

Being a Christian, I tried to keep my eyes focused on Jesus in all situations. There were times when things looked very bleak and my faith was weak, but one thing I know, that He promised in His Word that He would never leave or forsake me no matter how tough the times.

I was in a replacement company, attached to the Third Army. General George Patton was the Commanding Officer. We were there to replace those who were killed in battle and to face the enemy as we advanced.

I knew I had been assigned to the 839th Ordinance Depot Company. I had no idea where they were and they had no idea where I was. One day, we moved into a wooded area after we had passed Paris, France, about fifty miles. I found me a place in the forest where soft moss had grown on the ground that made a nice padding. I pitched my tent on this lovely mossy place. I was all set up and crawled in my tent to relax a bit. We had been encountering the enemy hostility during the day and traveling very slowly at night. I was very tired and the moss caused me to remember the old feather bed back home. I was lying there, praying, and thanking God for His protection as I listened to the sound of guns firing closely. The big artillery guns could be heard at a distance, as well as the sound of aircraft overhead, and the explosion of bombs. I had just dropped off to sleep, and I heard the harsh voice of our First Sergeant yelling out, "Lunsford, report immediately to the Company Tent." I wondered, "What now?" The Company Tent was only about fifty yards away, so I was there right away. He said, "Tear your tent down, and pack up to move out." A small Army truck was parked there with the 839th Ordinance Depot Company on the bumper. They had found me. I was replacing a young man that had been killed by a German booby trap. We headed north, seeing a lot of war-torn places along the way. After we had gone some distance, I saw my first German Buzz Bomb streaking across the pale blue sky. The Buzz Bomb was named by the American soldiers due to the harassing sound it made. This weapon was a guided missile, loaded with high explosives. It was set on a course so that when it was launched it had a particular target in mind. A jet-propelled engine drove it. When the fuel ran out, it fell to the ground and exploded when it hit the ground. Some of them were intended for London, England, others were for Belgium and Holland. Our anti-aircraft fighter planes could shoot them down, but wherever they hit, they caused mass destruction. However, the pilots of our P-51 Fighter Planes would fly up alongside the bomb when crossing the English Channel and take the tip of the wing of their plane and get it under the tip of the bombs' wing and flip it up, causing it to fall in the water. This was a very risky operation, but it worked to stop the destructive weapon from reaching England.

The next story I will share has to do with the singing nightingale. I hope you enjoy it.

Singing in the Dark
Acts 16:25

General Patton's 3rd Army was moving swiftly across France. The troops had to really keep on the move to fulfill their duty. A Company moved into a field late one night. The Captain told them not to pitch their tents, but to unroll their sleeping bags and get a little sleep. They would move out at daybreak the next morning. It was a warm summer night, the sky was clear, revealing a star-studded canopy. Two young men just nineteen years old were lying side by side. One was looking into the beautiful sky thinking about home. His heart was sad and lonely. Tears puddled up in his eyes and trickled down into his ears. The night was so dark, but his heart was even darker, wondering what the battle would be like tomorrow. He was bone tired from the very vicious battles in the past days. He heard a sound in the dense darkness of a hedgerow nearby. It sounded like beautiful music. Could it be he was allowing his mind to ramble and imagine the sound of music in the dark? But then he heard it again. Now it was more clearly. His buddy was now sound asleep. He reached over and shook him and said, "Listen." "Listen to what?" was the reply. They listened together, and the singing seemed to get louder. The machine guns were chattering nearby and the artillery guns in the distance did not sound so loud anymore. He said to his friend, "What is that?" His friend replied, "It is a nightingale. They sing only in the dark." The nightingale is a migratory bird that is noted for singing beautiful music in the dark. The darker the night, the more they sing.

One night, Paul and Silas were in the Philippian Jail, bound with chains; blood was oozing out of the wounds that were as red as spring roses. Their bruises were as purple as dahlias in the late fall. The prison was cold and damp and as dark as midnight. They were praying and singing in the dark. I do not know what they were singing, but perhaps they were singing Psalm 23:1 and Psalm 23:4, "The Lord is my Shepherd, I shall not want, Yea though I walk through the valley of the shadow of death, I will fear no evil: forThou art with me; Thy rod and Thy staff they comfort me." I am sure the jailer knew what had happened the day before as recorded in Acts 16:19-24. Paul and Silas were just doing what Christians are supposed to do. Some people didn't like it. They were arrested, beaten, and thrown in jail for preaching the Gospel. The jailer was charged with the responsibility of keeping the prisoners, murderers, thieves, and, of course, two preachers of the Gospel. These two prisoners were different, they were not complaining. They were indeed the fragrance of Christ to the other prisoners and the jailer. Of all things, they were singing in the dark. The prisoners heard them. I suppose they were saying to each other, "What is going on with these two fellows? They are different. Their stripes are bleeding, the stocks are hurting their ankles, chains are on their wrists, the prison is cold and dark, yet they are singing." No doubt, the Holy Spirit was moving in that prison. The jailer was asleep.

In 2006, five Amish girls, aged thirteen, were shot and killed by a man in Lancaster County, PA, who then killed himself. The event stunned the world. But what happened next stunned the world even more. A whole community was singing and praying, not bent on retaliation, shouting in anger, but standing with quiet dignity and calmness. The community was quick to forgive. They even established a charity fund for the killer's family. They faced the worst and became the best. Such peculiar people, singing in the dark.

Paul and Silas demonstrated deep abiding confidence in God, the God who is with us in the darkest of times.

We are all Here

The jailer had fallen asleep. Maybe the singing lulled him into a deep sleep. He is awakened abruptly by a mighty shaking. An earthquake was occurring that was powerful enough to fling the prison doors open, strong enough to shake prisoner's chains and stocks loose. The jailer is now wide-awake, stunned by what has happened. He knows that if his prisoners have escaped, his own life is on the line. He knows the noble thing to do is to kill himself, so he draws his sword. Paul shouted to him, "Don't harm yourself, we are all here." The jailer immediately falls on his knees pleading, "What must I do to be saved?"

Why would these men that have been treated so badly care about the jailer who was their enemy? What peculiar people! What power could make anyone behave this way? Nothing more or less than the dynamic power of God that is available to every believer if we sing in the dark.

Transfixed. Then there are the fellow prisoners sitting with no chains, no stocks, and no locked doors restraining them. They are all there. Why don't they flee? Something has riveted them to their seats. This power has astonished everyone. All were amazed at the grace of God in action to deliver His people. Revival had come to the jailhouse at the darkest hour because God's men dared to sing in the dark. The jailer sees the prisoners going nowhere. These hardened criminals suddenly acted against their most entrenched instincts. It was all because of the power of God in two men. Being saved means the saving of ones' soul, but it also includes knowing a God who defeats the powers of darkness and at the same time makes us willing to forsake our own freedom for the sake of others.

A Glimpse of Transformation. The jailer cried, "What must I do to be saved?" This must be the cry of all people in order for them to go to heaven. The question must be asked. The answer came loud and clear from a child of God whose body was racked with pain, and whose mind and heart was shrouded with darkness of rejection, punishment, and disappointment. And they said, "Believe on the Lord Jesus Christ, and thou shalt be saved and thine house." Let us never, in the name of our fashion, fad, or theology, make the Gospel anything other than this. It is the saving of the soul, but it is also the transforming of the life. Please note Acts 16:33-30-"And he took them the same hour of the night, and washed their stripes; and was baptized, he and all of his, straightway. And when he had brought them into his house, he set meat before them, and rejoiced, believing in God with all his house." So it is the saving of one's life to the point of revealing to others about the possibility of their own transformation that makes the difference.

Singing in the dark can indeed bring about a great revival. There has been so many times in my life that in my heart, I have sung in the dark although I do not have the gift of singing as that of many others. Thank God, we can sing even though darkness is all about us. "Well glory!"

THE BATTLE OF THE BULGE

I joined the 839th Ordinance Depot Company in Holland right on the front line. Our job was to help the Ninth Army that had just arrived from the United States to set up a supply depot to furnish needs for battle. Once that was accomplished, we moved to Belgium to join the First Army, at the Forward Field Depot. We would go right on the front line and move again when the line moved twelve miles. So we were on the constant move, encountering the enemy as we went. Many German snipers were hiding, ready to pick us off. Mines and booby traps were a great danger. We were moving slowly through Belgium, when on December 16th, 1944, the German's launched their attack along the front in Belgium and Luxembourg, bringing together twenty-five divisions, an essential of the German plan, put there by Hitler, himself. The plan was that continued mystery terror and confusion would beset the crumbling allied rear. The weather was bitter cold with snow and ice. On December 22, came the high drama of the closed siege. The German Corps Commander called on the Bastogne Garrison to surrender. The United States Commander, Anthony C. McAuliffe, replied, "Nuts," a message considered by some to be as famous as "Don't give up the ship," or "I have not yet begun to fight."

We were in the heat of the battle day and night. We were charged with the responsibility of keeping the front line supplied with necessary parts for vehicles, guns, and vehicles, themselves. One day, a young Lieutenant came in with a requisition for all of the tank destroyers we had in the motor pool. I knew he was from the 7th Armored Division in a Light Tank Company. I asked him why the tank destroyers? He said, "You will hear about it." The Germans were attacking us with all they had and in so doing, to our dismay; they were on the offensive, pushing us back. We were trying to defend our positions. This Company, being a Light Tank Company, had their light tanks on the line, armed with 35-millimeter guns. The Germans knew this, of course, and prepared to wipe out our line of defense. But when dark came that evening, our wise and well trained men took their light tanks off of the line and placed the tank destroyers, with their 90 millimeter guns and heavy armor, on the line. When the Germans came just after midnight, our men plastered them with 90-millimeter guns instead of 37-millimeter light tanks, repelled them, and drove them back. This is just one incident where our strategy and good equipment gave us the victory in the end. We were upon the front where all the fighting was going on, and things looked quite bleak for us. We had been given orders to prepare to set fire to all of our equipment and flee on foot as necessary. We had twenty-seven large vans loaded with all kinds of necessary items for battle. Three days and nights went by with battles raging. Aircraft, both friendly and enemy, were in the air. Sleep was impossible. After three days and nights, I had gone to sleep, after praying and making a promise to my God, that if He would bring me back to the mountains of Western, North Carolina, I would serve Him. I would do anything He wanted me to do and go anywhere He wanted me to go. After sleeping a little while, my Sergeant was shaking me and telling me we were moving out. We loaded our equipment and headed out in the night. We had to cross a river on a low bridge. The Germans were dropping flares to light up the place and then bombs to try to knock out the bridge. We got across, but there was a truck behind us that received a direct hit from a bomb, and some of the men in the truck went into the river. I heard a soldier crying out from the river below, "Help, help, I am going down." and then I heard him no more. We got out of the trap the Germans had set about one hour before they closed the gap.

We moved into a town in Belgium called Saint Tronde. While there, I had a big and very pleasant surprise. We had moved into a building that had been a mental hospital. It gave us protection from the bitter cold and snowy weather. Late one evening, I was lying on my little Army cot when I heard a familiar voice in the doorway that I hadn't heard in many months. The voice did not call the name, "Fred," but a family nickname, "Cooter." I looked and to my utter amazement, there stood my brother-in-law, Willard Greene. He was my wife's brother, serving in the Combat Engineers. They had been in battle for a long period of time and had come back for a brief rest period. He was close to the Mail Distribution Center, and he saw a mail truck with the 839th Ordinance Company on the bumper. He talked to the driver, asking him if he knew me and he told him he did. He asked him if he could get a pass if he would let him ride with him and bring him back the next day so he could visit with me and he said he would be glad for him to do so. He spent the night with me and went back the next day. What a wonderful blessing that was.

On New Years Day, 1945, a group of us were walking a short distance down a road to the motor pool where we had a large number of vehicles stored that had been evacuated out of the Bulge. These included everything from tanks to jeeps. It was a beautiful, sunshiny, morning. It was bitter cold, but the skies were clear. The sun was shining on the fresh fallen, white, snow. Ice tags were shining on the twigs and looked like diamonds. Everything was quiet and peaceful. Then all of a sudden, an American P-51 Fighter Plane came out of nowhere and began to strafe us with machine gun fire. I jumped into a foxhole to get away from the bullets that were hitting all around me. I had just barely got in the hole, when one of my comrades jumped in on top of me and said, "My God." He had said before that he was an atheist. I said, "You called on God that you said didn't exist." We prayed to God together in the foxhole. Following the P-51 were the German Fighter Planes. Our anti-aircraft fire began to shoot them down. They hit the P-51 and it caught fire and the pilot, a German, bailed out. His parachute opened and he glided to the snow- covered ground. There was a group of Belgium men waiting for him when he hit the ground. They cut his throat and stripped him of all he had and left his bare body lying in the blood-sprinkled, snow. The Germans had captured one of our Air Stripes in the Bulge and took possession of our P-51 Plane. I watched all of this and looked to the heavens and prayed. I thought, why war anyway, how cruel it is. This event was the last big push of the German Air Forces. Our troops stopped the German Army, pushed them back all the way to the Rhine River, and beyond. Thus, the Battle of the Bulge was over, but not without a terrible cost to us. Seventy-six thousand, eight hundred and ninety Americans were killed. God was so good to me to bring me through this terrible event. "Well glory!"

Southern France and Germany

We left the First Army and went to Southern France and joined the Seventh Army. We crossed the Rhine River at Worms, Germany, and pushed our way all the way to Pennsburg, Germany, right on the Austrian border in the foot of the Alp Mountains. We were traveling in a tractor-trailer rig loaded with tires, and met a road full of German soldiers. They scared me out of my wits. The only weapons we had were our primary weapons. We both had Thirty Caliber Carbines, and I had a Side Arm, a Forty-Five-Caliber Pistol. When they got closer, we discovered that the leader was a German officer who had a white handkerchief tied on a stick waving it. They were surrendering to us. We directed them to a POW Concentration Camp a few miles down the road. Pennsburg was a beautiful place where we could see the towering snow capped Alp Mountains piercing the majestic, blue, sky. The fresh, cold, streams were flowing in the dense forest nearby filled with the brown trout. There were lush green fields dotted with farmhouses with beautiful cattle and horses grazing, and herds of deer could be seen late in the evening along the edges of the fields. May 7, 1945, things were going as usual. My department was tires, tubes, batteries, battery acid, and welding gases. A truck pulled in to get a load of tires. I looked at his orders. Everything was in order and we were loading him up. Our First Sergeant came running out yelling that Germany had surrendered. Our work immediately slowed down. There was no fighting and the battle was over.

Some have asked me if I ever saw General George Patton in person. My encounter with this famous General was not exactly a pleasant one. We had crossed the Rhine River on a pontoon bridge at Worms and were camped some distance in Germany. The engineers on the front line had run out of gas for welding. We had no gas either, so one other man and myself took a truck and went several miles back to pick up some at a depot. We got on the Autobahn, the famous German super highway that was comparable to our interstates today. We acquired our cargo and were on our way back, trying to get back before dark, but a fan belt broke on our truck. We always carried a spare one, so we proceeded to fix it. We had just finished the job and were fixing to get on our way when we saw a command car coming down the big four-lane highway. I saw stars on the front of it, and I knew it was a General. It went by us but stopped and backed up. A big rough looking man got out. It was General Patton. We came to attention and saluted him. We were standing at attention and he stormed out, "What are you doing stopped here?" I said, "We broke a fan belt, Sir." He then replied, "It is funny to me that these things always happen at a beer joint." We had not even noticed that there was a German beer joint nearby. I just reached over and picked up the broken fan belt and held it up. He said, "As you were soldiers," and he got in his car and went on. We breathed a sigh of relief and went on our way.

The War is Over

We spent a few days at Pennsburg after peace was signed and then loaded all of our stuff up and headed back to Shorndorf, Germany. We sat up a pool for leftover war materials. In July, they loaded us on a train and we headed back into France. We were in route three days and nights, spending a lot of time stopped, waiting for other trains to pass by. We ended up in Marcella, France with orders to go to the South Pacific. We prepared our equipment and loaded it onto a cargo ship, which sailed out to Manila. We were scheduled to load onto a ship going to Manila on August 16. While waiting, I was walking guard duty about midnight on August 14. I heard ships blowing their horns in the harbor, guns firing, and there was a lot of commotion. A Military Police came along in a jeep and stopped and told me Japan had surrendered. We went ahead and loaded on the ship, the General A. E. Anderson, which was scheduled to go to Manila. We had just gotten on board and a cable message came from Washington for us to come home instead of going to the Pacific on a delay in route with a thirty-day leave. I arrived at Marble by bus on September 2 at 6:00 a.m. from Fort Bragg, N. C. I had sent my wife a telegram from New York telling her I would be home in a few days. The message said, -August 20, 1945-"Arrived in New York, will see you in a week or so." I got off the bus, put my old duffel bag on my back, and started walking the four miles to our Vengeance Creek home. I had a first cousin that lived about one-half of a mile from Marble who had a pulp- wood truck. I stopped at his house and he took me to where the school buses turned around about one-fourth of a mile from my home. My brother, Hoyt, who was eleven years younger than myself, was waiting on the school bus. He went running up the hill to tell them that I was coming. My wife had spent the night there waiting for me to arrive. She came running over the top of the hill. I saw her coming and I threw my duffel bag down and ran to meet her. What a reunion it was. "Well glory!"

While home for thirty days, they mailed me a fifteen-day extension and then I went back to Fort Bragg, North Carolina, and they gave me another twenty days. After those twenty days, I went back and they discharged me on November 16, 1945. "Well glory!"

Thank God for His goodness. I try to tell Him every day how much I love Him and how I thank Him for His wonderful blessing.

THE RING FOR THE RETURNING PRODIGAL
LUKE 15:22

At the wedding altar, the bridegroom puts a ring upon the hand of his bride, signifying love and faithfulness. Trouble may come to the household, the carpets may go, the pictures may go, the piano may go, everything else may go, but the marriage ring stays because it is sacred.

In the burial hour, the ring is withdrawn from the hand and kept in a safe place. Sometimes at anniversary time, the box is opened and as you look at the ring, there is room for a thousand sweet recollections of the golden ring.

When we are saved, Christ receives our soul into His keeping. He puts on it a marriage ring. He endows you at that moment with all of His wealth. You are one in Christ and the soul is one in sympathy, one in affection, and one in hope. There is no power on earth or of hell that can effect a divorcement after Christ and the soul are united. Kings have turned out their companions when they got tired of them, but Christ is the Companion that is true forever. Having loved you once, He loves you forever. Once they tried to divorce Margaret, a Scotch girl, from her Savior, Jesus. They said: "You must give up your religion." She said, "I can't give up my religion." So they took her down to the beach at the seashore and they drove in a stake at the low water mark, tying her to it expecting that as the tide came up, her faith would fail. The tide began to rise, coming up higher and higher to her waist, to her neck, then to her lips, and in the last moment, just as the waves were washing her soul into glory, she shouted the praises of Jesus.

Oh no, you cannot separate the soul from Jesus. It is an everlasting union. Battle, storm, and darkness cannot do it. Is it too much exaltation for a man who is but dust and ashes like myself to cry out both now and forever? "I am persuaded that neither height, nor depth, nor principalities, nor powers, nor things present, nor things to come, nor any other creature shall separate me from the love of God, which is in Christ Jesus, my Lord." Glory be to God when Christ and the soul are united, a golden chain with but one link, the link of God's everlasting love, binds them.

I go a step further and say that when Christ receives a soul into His love, He puts on her or him, "the ring of festivity." The old man in the story of the prodigal son wanted to make merry because his son was home. Before he ordered sandals put on his feet and before the fatted calf was killed, he commanded, "Put a ring on his hand." He was the reason for the festivity. Oh it is a merry time and what a splendid thing it is to know that all is right between my God and myself. What a glorious thing it is to have God just take up all my sins, put them in a bundle, and then fling them into the depths of the sea never to rise again and never to be mentioned again. All pollution is gone forever. Darkness is now light, reconciliation has occurred between God and me. The prodigal is home.

Down through the years, I have always found happy people. Some of them are with bare necessity of clothing, some with not enough food, some sick and forsaken, yet happy although they don't have earthly comforts. God says in His Word that He will never leave us or forsake us. "Well glory!"

I have said all of this to say the greatest thing that ever happened to me during these many years of travel was the day I trusted Jesus as my Savior. In a mountain revival meeting being held in a little one-room school house at the age of thirteen, I claimed Jesus as mine and He claimed me as His and life has been a celebration with Jesus since then. Sometimes the journey is uphill, dark, and stormy, but He is always there to own, to bless, lead, and empower for the journey.

Much has been said about religion in the Southern Appalachian Region. Volumes have been written about it, with most of it having been from a critical viewpoint, stereotyping us as ignorant mountain people.

As a testimony of one who grew up in these hills and served God among the mountain people, I must say that some of the greatest people in the world are the native mountain people in Western North Carolina, North Georgia, East Tennessee, and all over the Appalachian Region as for that matter.

I have traveled far and wide and studied different cultures. I am aware that mountain people are clannish, but life in the mountains demanded that the community had to support each other for survival. During my generation and the generations before me, people cared about each other. If a neighbor got his house burned, the rest of the community bonded together and helped build it back.

Everybody had a milk cow so they could have milk for the family. When the cow was dry, the neighbors furnished milk. Everyday, children had milk. No one posted his land. We hunted or fished anywhere we wanted to. Love was the one thing that dominated the activities. Togetherness, instead of individualism, was the norm.

Church was the center of the community, and the Bible was the guide to live by. No one needed to lock his door, because the Bible said we should not steal. Deep moral principles were instilled into the lives of the children. Religion was and is Christianity. One God, Jesus is the Savior, the Holy Spirit is the Guide and Power for the journey, and the Bible is the Word of God without the mixture of error.

Many years ago, I heard Dr. William Tanner, the President of the Baptist Home Mission Board; bring a message at Shoco Springs, Alabama on missions in the United States. He said when the Southern Baptist Convention started mission work in Ohio and Michigan and other points in the North; it was made much easier because many people during the thirties had migrated from the Southern Appalachian Mountains to find work. These people had taken with them their deep, religious culture that fleshed itself out in commitment, dedication, and hard work. I preached a revival in Dayton, Ohio where about two-thirds of the congregation were people from North Carolina, Tennessee, and Kentucky.

This mountain region has produced some of the nations' greatest religious leaders and educators. Many have gone out from these mountains to make outstanding contributions as College Professors, College Presidents, School Administrators, and Statesmen, as well as business leaders. One impact that these people have made is they have demonstrated a compassionate spirit of loving care for their fellow man. "Well glory!"

Most of the time, mountain people endure undue criticism for their expressions of worship rather that their dedicated puritan lifestyle. In another segment of this book, I include a message God gave me sometime ago on "Biblical Expressions of Worship." As I was studying for this message, I had some eye openers for myself. I bring to an end my remarks concerning this subject. I give forth a resounding, "Thank you to our

God, for my people who are called by many 'hillbillies,' but I call them wonderful God- loving, God-fearing, honest, hardworking people of the land." "Well glory!"

My Ministry Of Sixty Years

The Call to the Ministry

"And He said unto them, Go ye into all the world, and preach the gospel to every creature. He that believeth and is baptized shall be saved; but he that believeth not shall be damned."-Mark 16:15-16

I shall attempt to write about the awesome sixty years of ministry that the great God of the entire universe has blessed me with. It is all because of His marvelous grace. I trust that the things I share will bring honor and glory to God and not to me or any other man; however, many people have helped me through the years in the climbing of the mountains of life and enduring the valleys that I have often encountered. As I said earlier, I heard the famous singer and songwriter, Bill Gaither, say, "If you saw a turtle on top of a fence post, you can rest assured that he didn't get there by himself." It is a sure thing. I have been benefited by the goodness of many people along the way. It is still true everyday of my life and especially in these later days. So many friends bless me as they show forth their kindness and love toward my family and me.

I am reminded of the words of Wylie, a very dear friend from many years ago. Mr. King and his dear wife, Iva Lee, lived in our community just a short distance from us. For some years, my wife and I had a little country store across the road from our house. Uncle Wylie, as he was affectionately called, was legally blind and his hearing was about gone as well. Age and hard work had taken its toll on him and of course his wife, as well. These people were very godly people, providing faithful leadership in the little country church, which was located less than a half a mile, from where they lived. He had worked for the Southern Railroad, although he couldn't read and write. He drew a little railroad pension check each month and he depended on me to cash his check each and every month when it came in the mail. I was very glad to help in any way I could. I would often deliver groceries to them, as they had no children of their own. I loved them very much. I had known and appreciated them all of my life.

One day, I went to cash his check. He was sitting on the couch when I went in. I spoke to him as usual and we began a conversation. He said, "Come over here and sit by me." He patted the couch next to him. I sat down. He took both of those old wrinkled, weather-beaten, hands and reached over and put one on each side of my face and moved his face right up in mine and our noses were almost touching and said, "You know, I have known you all of your life. If I ever would have had the responsibility to pick out one person on this Creek to amount to anything for God, I would never have picked you. You are what you are by the grace of God, and more than that, you will go far and near, and God will use you in a mighty way. Always remember that I am praying for you and keep in mind that it is all because of God's marvelous and amazing grace." We both wept and prayed together, thanking God for grace.

When I came home out of the war, I got a job working in a store in Murphy, N. C., making thirty dollars per week for ten hours each day, working six days a week. We rented a little two-room house for twenty-five dollars per month. A few months later, we moved into an upstairs apartment that belonged to Ralph and Flonnie Deweese. I went to work for him, while taking schooling at the plumbing and pipefitting trade. I made sixty-five cents per hour and drew a check of ninety dollars each month from the Veterans Administration for my schooling. We moved to Vengeance Creek, living in a little house near where my dad lived. We were there when our first baby was born on October 2, 1947. The birth of this child changed our whole life. My wife was in labor thirty-six hours. In the middle of the night, I went out behind the hospital in the dark and got on my knees and prayed for my wife and my baby as earnestly as I knew how. I promised my God that I would keep my promise I made to Him while I was in the Battle of the Bulge. At 4:30 that next afternoon, he was born with the doctor's help. Shortly after his birth, we moved into a little four-room house by the side of the railroad track in the Pleasant Valley Community near Murphy, N. C. We joined Pleasant Valley Baptist Church, which had about twenty or twenty-five people in attendance at the time. Vengeance Creek Baptist Church had ordained me as a Deacon. When I joined Pleasant Valley Baptist Church, they elected me as a Deacon and then soon thereafter, they put me in as Sunday School Director. The pastor only came and preached one Sunday each month. He pastored three other churches. I prayed about the Sunday School. God directed me to do some things. One was to use my old pickup truck and haul some children and youth into Sunday School that wouldn't have the opportunity to come otherwise. God blessed our efforts and we soon had one hundred in our little Sunday School. We built some rooms for the classes with our own hands. God blessed every way we turned.

Then one day, the big event happened. I had always had a lot of respect for a preacher of the Gospel. As a child, when we were playing, sometimes we would play church and I always ended up being the preacher. When a puppy or a cat died at our house, my sister and myself would conduct a funeral. She would sing and I would preach the funeral. We would then bury the departed and place wild flowers on the grave. While in the army, I promised the Lord that I would do anything He wanted me to if He would only bring me home.

For sometime, I had been feeling like God wanted me to do something more, possibly to preach His Word, but I just brushed those inclinations aside, because after all, I was just an ignorant mountain boy. I couldn't do that, but one evening late, I went down the hill to the spring with two, ten-quart, water buckets to bring some water to have for the night and the next morning. We didn't have electricity. No one did in the rural area until R.E.A. came into being. I tried to carry up enough water for Gladys and our baby to have plenty while I was at work the next day. As I was walking up the hill with two buckets of water, it seemed to me that I heard a voice. I stopped and looked and no one was there, so I started trudging up the hill and I heard it again. I stopped and sat my water down that time and looked all around. I had heard about the Lord speaking to people but He had never spoken to me before that I knew of. I looked up into the heavens. It was a beautiful day. The sky was so blue and the sun was setting in the West. A cool evening breeze was blowing on my brow. I stood there trembling and said, "My Dear Lord, your servant is listening, if it is You, what do You want?" That sweet, penetrating, voice spoke to me, whether to the ear or to my heart, I know not, but I do know that I heard Him as He said, "Preach my Word." I stood there shaking like a leaf being blown by a brisk winter wind. I said, "Okay, Lord. I told you I would do anything." I went on to the house and told no one, not even my wife. Sunday came. I opened Sunday School and said as little as I could. All of this went on for about a month. Then one night, I woke up in the night and Gladys was heaving for breath. I got up and lit an old kerosene lamp.

I looked at her and her face was as blue as a faded pair of denim pants as she was trying to breathe.

I looked at little Dannie and he was sound asleep. I got on my knees and said to God, "I need your help. Please spare her, I love her, I need her to help me raise this baby. If it is preaching You want me to do, I am ready, but please answer my prayer." Then I felt the warmth and peace of God's presence like the rays of the warm morning sun. I looked and she was sitting up in the bed breathing normal and smiling at me.

The next Sunday after Sunday School was over, I asked everyone to be seated in the auditorium. I had something I wanted to say. I stood up trembling with tears running down my cheeks. I told them my story. "I am here and now announcing my call to preach God's Word." Everyone seemed to be so happy and Mr. Oscar Hensley said, "I knew it. I was waiting for you to admit it." That little group of godly, mountain people pledged to pray for me and God began to open doors for me to preach. I went back to my home church at Vengeance Creek and preached my first sermon. It lasted about five minutes. That has all changed now. The week before I preached at the church, I went to see Grandmother who was now bedfast. My mother was caring for her. I went in and said to her, "Grandma, God has called me to preach." She said, "Where is your Bible?" I said, "It is out there in my pickup truck." She said, "Go get it." I went and got it while thinking about a passage of Scripture that I might read to her. She often would ask me to do that because she couldn't read. I came back in the room with my Bible and she said, "I will never get to go hear you preach. So, I want you to preach to me." I replied, "Grandma, just you?" She said, "Yes, just me. Now, get on with it." So I read some Scripture and preached about five minutes. She shouted thirty minutes. Then she said, "All the time you were in the war, I prayed for you every day. I knew you would come back because when you were fourteen years old up in the June Apple Tree singing, God told me that you would preach His Word for many years." "Well glory!" I am now the same age she was when she died and still preaching His wonderful Good News.

I preached one year before I started pastoring churches. God blessed me with the opportunity to enroll in college classes at Epworth, Ga. I had the distinct privilege of riding with Rev. J. Alton Morris who was the Pastor of First Baptist Church of Murphy, N. C. He was one of the teachers. He was a former Professor at Mercer University. The classes were an extension of that school. Rev. Charlie Sexton was Pastor of Owl Creek Baptist Church. He only preached there two Sundays each month, so he set me up a standing appointment to preach on one of his off- Sundays. A man by the name of Jim McRae was the Sunday School Director. He took me in and encouraged and loved me. What a great man he was.

I started preaching in an old abandoned house in Fairview Community on Valley River on Sunday afternoons. People came from far and near during the summer months. So many people prayed for me and helped me along the way.

A new pastor was elected as pastor of Pleasant Valley Baptist Church. His name was Oliver Cornwell. He lived near us there in Pleasant Valley. This great man of God had a prayer altar up on the mountain near our house. I could hear him up there praying day and night, often calling my name in prayer. He is the man that ordained me and encouraged me in so very many ways.

A few days before he died, I went to see him. He was so frail and weak there in his bed. I stood at the foot of the bed holding on to the old iron bed stand. He looked at me and said, "Brother, Fred, I have never preached outside of Cherokee County, but I have prayed many prayers for you. You will preach far and near and see many souls saved and I will have a little part." It is so very true. Wherever I have gone in service for God, Brother Oliver has been there through me and will have his reward in heaven for his faithfulness.

Pastoral Ministry and God's Training Ground

A revival was being held at Pleasant Valley Baptist Church. The Rev. Ralph Matheson from Robbinsville was doing the preaching. Rev. A. B. Lovell, who was Pastor of Little Brasstown Baptist Church and Mt. Pisgah Baptist Church, came to the services two or three nights. On his last night, he asked me to go preach at Mt. Pisgah on one Sunday night. I readily agreed. I felt good that I had been asked, but as the time approached, I got increasingly afraid. It is a fearful thing to handle the Word of God. The time came for me to go. When I arrived, to my surprise, the hilltop, where the church building was located, was covered with people. To my utter amazement, Rev. Lovell was there. I thought he was going to be gone. Now I was really scared. To top it all off, the Clay County Sheriff was there. They sang and prayed and now it was time for me. I have no idea what I said or how I said it. If anything good was said, God had to do it. After the service was over, many people, as well as Rev. Lovell, were very kind, telling me how good I did. I knew better.

FRIENDSHIP

In a very short while, a group of people from Hiawassee, GA, came to my house to talk with me. When they arrived, they told me they were the Pulpit Committee for Friendship Baptist Church at Hiawassee, GA. They told me I had been recommended to them for Pastor and they would like for me to come to their church and preach and see what happened from there. I agreed to go, but I did a lot of praying before the time arrived. The church was a very small church. When TVA built Chatuge Dam, the water line of the lake came right up to the back of the church building. A lot of the people who went to the church had to sell their homes and move elsewhere. The meeting went good that day and they elected me half-time as their pastor. That meant that I would be with them every other Sunday or two Sundays per month. I found out that it was Brother A. B. Lovell who had recommended me. The church requested that the Pleasant Valley Baptist Church, where I was a member, ordain me to the Gospel ministry. They set a time for that to happen. The preachers that helped ordain me have long since gone on to be with the Lord. They were Rev. Oliver Cornwell, Rev. Ralph Matheson, Rev. Freed Townson, and Rev. Gordon Scruggs. This ordination took place on September 24, 1950.

During the time of this procedure, Little Brasstown Baptist Church elected me for two Sundays per month on the recommendation of Rev. Lovell, who had just left the church to go to Peachtree Memorial Baptist Church. Several years later, I asked him why he recommended me to those churches. He replied by looking at me as only he could with that little smile and said, "I have wondered the same thing, but now I know why. I am very proud of you." He was truly a great man of God. He was a great help to me in so very many ways.

My stay at Friendship Baptist Church only lasted for two years, but it was a great two years. The first summer I was there, they wanted me to preach a few nights' revival. Two young men were saved. They were Wayne and Josephine Galloways' two boys. They were the first two people I baptized. We had the Baptism Service on Sunday morning down at the lake. I just walked out on the pavement as deep as I needed to and baptized them. Since then, God has blessed me with the privilege of baptizing hundreds of people. While I was there I developed a relationship with Rev. John Greene. Brother Greene was one of the best-educated preachers in the mountains. He lived just across the line over in Georgia. I would go pick him up and bring him to my house and keep him for two weeks at a time and let him teach me the Bible. We would start in the morning about 8:00 and go until 9:00 that night. We would take time to eat and he would take a short afternoon nap. He said he needed his rest because he was then eighty-three years old, the same age I am now. He started me on my journey of learning and developing in God's Word. He went to Friendship Baptist Church to preach revival for a week. Large crowds would come to hear him because he was well known throughout North Georgia and Western North Carolina. He would only preach every other service. He insisted that I preach the other services. He had preached on Saturday night. It was my turn to preach on Sunday morning. People were gathering in on this beautiful sunshiny Sunday morning. The flowers were blooming. The birds were singing. Everybody looked so beautiful and I was excited. I could hardly wait 'til it was time for me to preach. I had studied, prayed, and thought I had a good sermon prepared. Some of us were talking in the churchyard under the big oak trees when a big shiny brand new Cadillac drove up and parked close by. I said to some of the men, "Who is that?" They said, "That is Senator Miligan from Atlanta. He has built a new summer home on the lake near here." I was the pastor, so my duty was to welcome all the visitors. I shook hands with him and told him whom I was and gave him a hearty welcome and then I realized that I was going to be preaching to this man. He was a Senator and Deacon in one of the largest churches in Atlanta. I went to Brother Greene and told him he would have to preach because I just couldn't. He replied with that commanding voice, "No, Freddie boy, it is your time, you will do the big boy well." When I got up to preach, the Senator was sitting on the front pew looking right up at me. My knees were shaking and perspiration was beading up on my brow. Chills were playing Yankee Doodle up and down my backbone. I said, "Let us pray." I called on Brother Charlie Phillips, the Senior Deacon, to lead us in prayer. While he was praying, so was I. I told God that I couldn't but He could and asked Him to take over and He did. I read the Scripture, and from there on I don't know what I said, but I heard a deep bass voice down front come out with a resounding, "A-Men!" I looked at Senator Miligan and tears were trickling down his cheeks. They looked like huge diamonds. After the service, he shook my hand and said, "Young man, you blessed my heart," and he handed me a check for one hundred-dollars made out to the church to help on our building repairs. He said, "I will be coming here to church when I am up here on the weekends. I will also give you some more money to help on this beautiful little building." What a blessing that wonderful Christian man was. The money really came in handy. Back then, one hundred-dollars was worth more than one thousand in today's economy. I thank God for the wonderful contribution that these dedicated Christian people made to my life and to the Kingdom of God.

After I had been serving with them as half-time Pastor for two years, I felt that I should go to Little Brasstown Baptist Church every Sunday, as well as whatever ministry I could provide, while working on a public job to support my family. I served this church as bi-vocational Pastor for ten years. I resigned Friendship Baptist Church with them begging me to stay. Mr. J. Y. Denton, a banker at Hiawassee, said, "There is no sense in this. Everybody wants you to stay and besides that, we will raise your pay." I said to him, "Isn't it much better for me to leave with your wanting me to stay, than for you wanting me to go and I wouldn't?" He thought for a moment and said, "I guess you are right." I did what I did because I knew I was doing God's will and it proved to be true. I left with a great love relationship with those lovely people. Most of them have now gone on to be with the Lord. I have gone back and had a part on many of their funeral services.

LITTLE BRASSTOWN

As I have already stated, I was elected as half-time Pastor of Little Brasstown Baptist Church. I began my ministry there the first Sunday in October 1950.

The Sunday I was voted in, a dear man in the church, by the name of Brother Luther Carringer, went to visit a friend, Mr. Theodore Cook. It was in the afternoon. Mr. Cook was not a member of Little Brasstown Church at the time, but a very highly respected citizen of the community and a devoted Christian. Luther visited for a little while and said to Mr. Cook, "We really messed up at Little Brasstown today." Theodore asked, "What did you do?" Luther answered, "We elected that Lunsford boy for our pastor and he can't preach a lick." Mr. Cook replied quickly to his friend, Luther's, statement of fear, "Luther, you better be careful what you say about that boy because God has His hand on his life." Luther said no more but went home and told his wife, Bertha, about what Mr. Cook said. She said, "Well, I agree with Mr. Cook. I have known Fred for many years, and I know he is God's man."

Luther told me about all of this and said, "Now I know that they were right and I was wrong. I love you more than I could ever say." He also told me that they elected me on trial for one year just to see how it worked out. At the end of one year, on one of my off- Sundays, they had Rev. Robert Barker, a noted Preacher of Western North Carolina, to fill the pulpit and voted me in as their Pastor for an indefinite period of time.

When I took over the leadership of this church, God was already blessing there under the leadership of an outstanding man of God, Brother A. B. Lovell. He was a great man to follow, although I could never fill his shoes.

The policy of the church was to have a college student summer worker, provided by the association to lead in Vacation Bible School. This went very well with fine results. One summer, sometime after I became pastor, I decided we could do it ourselves. We had a fine young man in the church, by the name of Lyle Carringer, who was a college student. I told him that he was going to lead our VBS that summer. He said, "Why I can't do that." I replied, "Oh yes you can. I will help you." He soon agreed and we went to work at it. We had a ten-day school from 9:00 a.m. until noon each day. We ended up with one hundred and fifty enrolled. For refreshments, we decided we would make real lemonade. It was necessary to buy one half of a bushel of lemons and a lot of sugar. Ralph and Betty Myers had a dairy farm, so they furnished us with two, ten –gallon, milk cans. I took on the responsibility of squeezing the lemons and stirring them with a wooden paddle as well as serving the children. The women made homemade cookies, enough for one hundred and fifty people each day. What a time we had. Several young people were saved and we all drew closer to God and each other. From that day to now, Little Brasstown has never had outside help for VBS.

There were so many wonderful things that brought glory and honor to God, and made me look good, but I know who was responsible for these mighty and beautiful years. It could never have happened had it not been for the gracious, dedicated, and committed people of the church.

Our church building was full and running over every Sunday. The structure was old, with termites invading the wood foundation and walls. I went to prayer meeting one Wednesday evening, arriving a little early before anyone else showed up. I went out in a wooded area near the church to have a little private talk with God as I often did. I came back out to the churchyard, and sat down on a stump, still communing with God. I looked out where I had been and saw in my mind a beautiful, new, church building standing there. The property where I had been praying did not belong to the church, but was owned by the John C. Campbell Folk School, which was located at the foot of the hill below the church. Just then, as I was gazing out into the dense forest, Ralph Myers came driving up the hill. He parked his vehicle and came over to me and spoke, asking what I was looking at. I told him what I was seeing. He said, "Let's build it." We had no money. No one had a lot of money. Most of the people in the church were farmers. There were a few school teachers and a few business people. The next week, I went to see Uncle Bill Clayton, who was the Chairman of the Deacons in the church. He was a very highly respected leader in the community. I asked Uncle Bill to go with me over to the church. We went in the educational space in the basement of the building. I showed him the sign of termites in the woodwork. I showed him the decaying of the foundation and pointed out that we were full every Sunday, therefore, we couldn't grow. He said what do you suggest that we do about it. I said, "Uncle Bill, we need a new church building." He looked off into the distance and whistled a little, as he often did when he was thinking. I had just launched on him an idea that was entirely foreign to him. After a while, he said, "This old building will do me as long as I will need a church building." I then said, "But, Uncle Bill, we have a lot of young people here, and they need a place to worship and to learn about Jesus." He in turn looked me right in the eyes, with a tear puddling up in his eyes and now trickling down his wrinkled face, and said, "You are our preacher. God sent you here to be our leader. So, if you think we need a new building, then I say we need a new building." I asked him if he would tell the congregation that on Sunday morning. He indicated that he would.

Sunday morning came. We had an unusually large crowd. The service was now over. I asked the people to be seated for a few minutes and told them that Brother Bill Clayton had something he wanted to say. He stood up at the front and said, with great clarity and a note of authority in his word, "As you can well see, our building is full. We cannot seat any more people. Our preacher thinks we need a new building. I agree with him because the termites are eating up this one. With this in mind, I want to start a Building Fund." He pulled a one hundred-dollar bill out of his pocket and laid it on the communion table. One hundred dollars in those days was a lot of money. A few pews back, Brother (Pappy) Bert Hogan, another Deacon, came out and down the aisle saying as he came, "If Bill Clayton can give one hundred dollars, so can I." He laid another one hundred-dollar bill on the table. Several other people gave smaller amounts. When we counted it, we had three hundred dollars in the Building Fund and voted to build a new building.

We went to the Folk School and they agreed to give some additional land to put the building on and the work began. We worked Saturdays and any other time we could, to do site preparation. No one had much money, but we all gave all we could and worked hard to build the Lord's house. Loy Payne, a very successful logger and saw miller, was saved in his fifties and I baptized him into the life of the church. He furnished his equipment to prepare the site. His son, Max, would run the bulldozer and some of his timber cutters would run the chain saws. When it was all over,

Loy had donated fourteen thousand feet of lumber and only God knows how many hours of work and money.

One of the Saturday workdays, when we were pouring the foundation, seven people showed up to help. There were four teenaged girls, June and Jane Logan, Liz and Edith Zimmerman, and three men, Uncle Bill Clayton, Marion Myers, and myself. The girls used shovels, loading the concrete mixer. Marion and myself rolled the concrete in wheelbarrows, and Uncle Bill cut the concrete. What a day we had.

Early on, during this building campaign, I got to know Dr. Dumont Clarke, through the Farmer's Federation, that headed up the "Lord's Acre Plan." I explained it to the congregation. Since most of them were farmers, they readily accepted the plan, which became a great success. A family would plant an acre of corn, a row of potatoes, beans, or any other garden produce. They might raise a pig or a calf. Many of the young people got involved in the program. We would go to the pigpen, calf barn, pasture or field, and have a dedication service on a given Sunday afternoon. Mrs. Cora Jones gave her Sunday eggs since she had a flock of chickens. She said when the old hens were cackling on Sunday, she just praised the Lord for the fact that they had laid more eggs on Sunday than any other day of the week. I have wondered if her husband, Alec, left a few on Saturday evening in order to make more on Sunday.

When they took the livestock to the auction on Tuesdays, Marion Myers or Bill Clayton would tell the auctioneer that calf number ten, or whatever the number might be, was a Lord's Acre calf. He would then tell the buyers what it was for, and he would run the price as high as he could. Many little things that occurred during those days were great blessings.

In the fall, we would have a harvest day and people would bring the proceeds from their project and lay it on the altar and we would celebrate God's wonderful blessings. Many would share testimonies as to how they had received tremendous blessings from having had the privilege of producing something for the glory of God.

Three years after we started the building, we moved into our new worship center and educational facility. Rev. A. B. Lovell, a former Pastor, came and preached the first revival in the new building. At the close of the revival, I baptized twenty-five new converts.

The first ten years of my ministry as Pastor of Little Brasstown, I was a bi-vocational Pastor. The church grew as God blessed us with many new members. The last years of the ten, the church leadership began talking to me about quitting my job with Berkshire Knitting Mills at Andrews, and devoting my full time as their Pastor and doing evangelism. I told them I would resign and let them call a full-time Pastor and they in turn replied with an affirmative, "No." If I wouldn't take it, we would go on like we were. I prayed much about it. I was preaching a lot of revivals in other churches during this time. One summer, I preached thirteen weeks every night, worked fifty hours per week, and pastored the church. As I look back on it now, I know God had to give me added strength to do all of that.

One day, the Superintendent of the mill where I worked, called me in the office to meet with him and the mill supervisors. He told me that the plant was going through a big transition and my job was going to be phased out. They wanted to transfer me to another department and this would require me to go to Pennsylvania for six weeks of schooling and I would have to take a cut in pay. I said, "Mr. Gernert, I appreciate all you have done for me these years that I have been working here and what you are trying to do for me now, but I quit!" He said, "What are you going to do?" I said, "I am going into full-time ministry." He then asked all the others to leave the room where he could talk to me alone. He looked at me as only he could with those piercing eyes. He said, "Fred, not everyone believes like we do, but I believe the Bible is true, therefore, all things work together for good to those who love the Lord and are called according to His purpose. I believe you love the Lord and I further believe you are called of God to the ministry. If you will stay with me six more weeks and finish the project you have started in the machine shop, then you can go with my blessings and I will pray for you." Thus, I began my journey as a full- time minister that has lasted almost half a century.

While I was working with Berkshire, the Superintendent, Mr. S. J. Gernert, a very fine man, told me he wanted me to go to Virginia for two weeks with a crew of men to take some machinery out of a plant that they had bought. The machines were needed at the Andrews plant. The initial crew that went was Ray Hogsed, Harry Hawk, Glenn Holloway, L. B. Hardin, N. L. Adams, and myself. I got someone to fill in for me at the church the one Sunday we were to be gone. The second week we were there, the Company officials came down from Reading, PA. and asked to meet with me. They bought me a steak supper and told me they wanted me to stay there and take all of the machinery out of the building, sending some to Andrews, some to Reading, and shipping some to an overseas plant and scrapping some which would take about three months. I told them that I was the Pastor of a church and that I had to be there to preach on Sunday. I told them I felt the Lord's work had to come first. They told me

I could drive the Company station wagon, leave Andrews at 4:00 a.m. on Monday and leave Virginia on Saturday at noon and they would pay me one way as well as the whole crew. That way, I could preach at the church on Sunday. The church agreed to this arrangement and so we worked this way for three months, finishing the project, with a deep bonding of love and friendship that still exists today. N. L. Adams and Glen Holloway have now gone on to be with the Lord. L. B. Hardin is retired and lives in Andrews, N. C. Rev. Harry Hawk became a Methodist Minister, pastoring churches in North Carolina, including the First United Methodist Church of Bryson City, N. C. He is now retired and living in Andrews, N. C. Ray Hogsed served two different times on the City Council of Andrews and then retired as an employee of the city. He now lives in Andrews at the age of eighty-three.

Grouse Hunting

While serving as Pastor of Little Brasstown, a man by the name of Robert Don Kephart built a house in the community. When the house was completed, he and his family moved in and started attending Little Brasstown Baptist Church. About the same time, Melvin Crisp joined the church as a candidate for baptism. I had the joyous experience of baptizing him. I started hunting and fishing with Don (some called him Robert) and Melvin, as well as trout fishing and lake fishing, now and then. We walked hundreds of miles together, hunting mountain grouse with Don's bird dog, Princess, and later her pup, Queen. We missed more birds than we killed, but we did get our part. Sometimes, we would go hunting and our wives would get together with the children at one of our homes and fry up a bunch of grouse and make gravy and biscuits along with a lot of other good vittles to have when we got in from a hard day of hunting. My what a good time we had. Don's brother, Ralph, who lived in Lexington, N. C. would come and go with us now and then. Later on, Lawrence Hogsed, whom I baptized, also joined in on the hunts as well. He has now gone on to be with the Lord as well as Melvin Crisp. Don is now a shut in.

Blessed Years of Association Missions

In November of 1963, God was blessing the work with Little Brasstown Baptist Church. The Church wanted to pay my way to the meeting of the North Carolina Baptist State Convention, which was meeting at Wilmington, N. C. on the Carolina Coast that year. Three other Pastors, Rev. Thad Dowdle of Marble Springs Baptist Church, Rev. Don Turner of Truett Memorial Baptist Church, and Rev. Jessie Bailey of Mt. Pleasant Baptist Church, went with me. We made arrangements to stay at the Caswell North Carolina Baptist Assembly to save money. We slept in bunk beds, all in the same room. When we got in from the meeting at night, we would have a prayer meeting before going to bed. We surely had a great week in the Lord. We were blessed beyond measure. On our way back home, we decided we would start a Monday morning Pastor's Prayer Meeting. When we got home, we had a meeting with our Association Missionary, Rev. Elmer Green, and discussed it with him. He liked the idea so we began meeting on Monday morning at 10:00 a.m. at one of the churches, rotating it from church to church. This has now been going more than forty years and is still going. Brother Greene, our Missionary, went to a Statewide Vacation Bible School Clinic at Wingate College in January of 1964. While there, he had a massive heart attack and went on to his reward. At that point, I was serving on the Association Missions Committee. It was the responsibility of the Missions Committee to find a replacement for Elmer.

We began looking and praying concerning who God would have in this position of leadership. We looked at several people but all the doors were closed. Richard Powers was the Chairman of the Committee. He was a Public Accountant, maintaining his office in Hayesville, N. C. We had a meeting of the Committee set for Monday night at First Baptist Church in Murphy, N. C. He called me that morning and asked me to come to his office. On arrival, he asked me to have a seat. I sat down and we chatted for a few minutes and he looked across the desk at me and said, "Would you be willing to leave Little Brasstown Baptist Church and take the position of Association Missionary?" I was shocked that he would say such a thing to me. It had not even entered my mind. I replied, "No." We talked a few minutes longer, and then he had a client come in, so I left.

We arrived at the Church for the meeting that night at 7:00 p. m. My friend and Deacon, Don Kephart of Little Brasstown Baptist Church was also on the Committee. All Committee members were present and Richard was presiding over the meeting. After having prayer, he asked if anyone had any suggestions concerning someone to fill the position of Association Missionary. Rev. Jimmy Rogers, Moderator of the Association, said, "I do. He is sitting right over there." He pointed at me. Richard said, "Fred, what do you say?" I said, "No." They asked me to leave the room. I went out in the church sanctuary and sat down in the dark. I tried to pray, but it was so difficult. After a long time, it seemed to me forever, they came after me. They told me, "We have decided that you are the man for the job. We will give you two weeks to pray about it and then you can give us an answer. We will have another meeting two weeks from tonight." Then we had a closing prayer. Don Kephart and I had carpooled from his house that evening. As we went on back up the road that night, very little was said. He finally said, "You are my Pastor. I love you, therefore, I can't vote for you to take this job, although I know that God would use you in this work."

I prayed for two weeks, sleeping very little. I really wanted to stay at Little Brasstown Baptist Church. In my praying, I asked God to save someone in the church on the following Sunday if He wanted me to stay there. It was not uncommon for someone to be saved. The church was really growing. God was blessing. Sunday came and it was a beautiful day. The people were gathering. A man met me when I arrived and said to me, "There is the man that I have been praying for such a long time. He is here this morning. I believe he will be saved today." I knew this was my answer that I wouldn't have to leave. The service went well that morning with a large crowd and a Great Spirit. I preached and gave the invitation as usual. Our man that I was sure would come forward, making a profession of faith, was sitting near the back of the building. He started moving out of his pew into the aisle. I thought this is great. Here he comes, but when he got out in the center aisle, he stopped, looked at me, turned around, and walked out the door. I had my answer. I knew I had to go, but I kept praying all the next week. The next Sunday morning before daybreak, I was in my living room on my knees. I told the Lord that I was ready to go anywhere He wanted me to go and to do anything He wanted me to do. It seemed to me that the hand of God touched me and I got relief. That Sunday at church, Daisy Myers, the great prayer warrior, said to me, "I don't like it, but I know you are gone." On the following Monday night, I went to the Committee Meeting and told them if the Association wanted me as their leader, I would try to do my best.

They called a special meeting at Shady Grove Baptist Church in Hayesville, N. C. to have a vote. I didn't go to the meeting, but they told me that a large crowd of people showed up and gave me a unanimous vote. I resigned the church, giving them a thirty-day notice. I began my work as missionary with the Western North Carolina and West Liberty Baptist Association on April 20, 1964.

The two associations covered all of Cherokee and Clay Counties. I agreed to handle both associations for the rest of the year. After that, I would have only the Western North Carolina Association. It included all of Clay County and about half of Cherokee County, North Carolina. There were thirty-two member churches in the Western North Carolina Association while West Liberty had fifteen churches from just West of Murphy, North Carolina to the Tennessee and Georgia lines.

In the fall of 1964, West Liberty Association elected Rev. Willard D. Graham; a very fine dedicated Pastor in the Association to be their Missionary. We worked together very closely in ministry to the churches in whatever way they needed us. We traveled together to training conferences and conventions across the State. On one occasion, we had been to Raleigh, N. C. to a meeting and were on our way home, traveling on I-85 at Charlotte at 5:30 in the evening. It was raining. We had experienced a long dry spell so that meant, since the rain had just started, that there was an oil slick on the road. I was driving behind a big truck without a trailer at about fifty-five miles per hour. I started to pass him and just as I did, he cut over in front of me to pass someone in front of him. I hit my brakes and went into a skid, sliding around twice in the road among that Charlotte rush-hour traffic. We went out in the medium, hit some large shrubs and turned over on our side. I was lying on top of Mr. Graham. He was short man and much of the time I called him "Little man." I said, "Little man, are you hurt?" He said, "I don't know until you get off the top of me so I can breath." Just then, looking up, I saw the car door open. A man was standing on top of the car holding the door open, extending me his hand to help me out of the car. He then helped "Little man" out. The good man who helped us was driving a big rig behind us. He said he did all he could to keep from hitting us. We just barely got out of his path in time. A State Trooper came right away. He called a wrecker, which got us back on our wheels. We drove down the road to a service station where we got the car checked out, adding some oil and transmission fluid. The attendant asked if we were the ones that turned over down the road. We told him we were. He said, "You fellows must be paying the preacher. You just don't have an accident like that at 5:30 in the evening and walk away." Brother Graham said, "We are the preachers." The attendant laughed and said, "What kind of preachers are you. I want to get on your side." We drove the car on home, thanking God for His care. When the insurance adjuster came and looked at the car, he said, "You are supposed to be dead. I read the accident report at Charlotte during the rush hour traffic." God, in His Word, promised us that He would never leave or forsake us. I claimed that promise a long time ago, and He has kept His promise. I expect that He will be with me all the way home. Rev. Graham went on to be with the Lord in old age, leaving behind a great testimony for God.

My job description called for helping all churches, regardless of their size. I grew up in Vengeance Creek Baptist Church, which was very small. As a child, I went to church in a little one-room schoolhouse heated with an old wood-burning heater. We had Sunday School every Sunday, but the Pastor only came one Sunday per month. He preached on Saturday at 11:00 a. m. and conducted the business meeting, which was called, "Conference." He would spend the night with a family in the community and preach on Sunday at 11:00 a. m. The standing culture of the worship style of the church was highly emotional. Most of the small mountain churches were this way. It was a common thing for some of the ladies to shout praises to God and it was expected that the men would give the preacher a hearty, "Amen," now and then.

When I started preaching and became Pastor of Little Brasstown Baptist Church, it was much different. Seldom did anyone shout. The men would "A-men" the preacher only once in a while. Now, I had to adjust to all expressions of worship, which was not hard for me to do. However, many people were critical of others who did not express themselves in worship the way they did or in the way they were accustomed to.

Some years later, God led me to preach a sermon on Biblical expressions of worship. This was a real eye-opener to me because there were some expressions that some used that I was uncomfortable with myself. I will briefly share some of the revelation I received from God's Word on this subject in the next few pages.

Scriptural Expressions of Worship

In John, chapter 4, Jesus encountered a woman who had come to draw water from Jacob's Well at Sychar. She said, to Him in verse 20-21, "Our fathers worshipped in this mountain; and ye say, that in Jerusalem is the place where men ought to worship. Jesus saith unto her, Woman believe me, the hour cometh, when ye shall neither in this mountain, nor yet at Jerusalem, worship the Father." In verse 24, it says, "God is a Spirit: and they that worship Him must worship Him in spirit and in truth."

Each and every Sunday morning or sometimes at other times, two kinds of people gather in places of worship. People go to church for a variety of reasons. It may be that they go out of duty. No doubt, some go for fellowship to see and to be seen. Then, there are those who assemble to worship God.

Worship is our response to the divine, loving, caring, God. It is never boring. Worship is never to be a time of entertainment.

A young lad of a boy was once boarding a plane with his parents with anticipation of visiting his Grandparents in a distant city. As he came aboard, he was heard saying with a loud commanding voice, "I want to see the pilot." They tried to calm him, but he kept saying, "I want to meet the pilot." The pilot heard him as his high pitched, youthful, voice vibrated through the large aircraft. The pilot came out of his cabin and said, "Does someone want to see me?" The boy said, "Are you the pilot of this big plane?" He said, "Yes I am, Son. What do you want?" The little fellow, with his voice trembling with deep emotion, said, "I just wanted to meet the pilot of this great ship. It is so wonderful to hear your voice and to see your face." The good captain took the little boy by the hand and led him gently to the cabin, sat down on his seat, and lifted the little boy up in his lap. He showed him the flight panel with all the instruments and gauges and gave him a set of wings to wear on his shirt and said, "I am your friend," as he escorted him back to his parents. After he got seated, he looked up into his mother's face and said, "I met the pilot." Their flight soon ended and they got off the plane. Waiting for them at the terminal, were his grandparents. He ran up to them with his face beaming and with a voice of excitement said, "I met the pilot."

People on a flight and people in churches are all on a journey. When we gather to worship, our absolute purpose should be to meet our Pilot, our Captain, our Master, and our Savior, Jesus Christ. How we react to this encounter is our own business and how someone else reacts to meeting with the Captain is none of our business.

When we have a worship experience, our reaction or expression may be different from our next-door neighbor's.

There are many Scriptural expressions of worship. We shall look at a few of them. I am aware that some of these may make us a bit uncomfortable because of our culture. Psalms 95:6 says, "O come let us bow down: let us kneel before the Lord, our Maker." Some churches have kneeling rails on the back of their pews. They practice kneeling in the congregation. Others go to the altar at the front to kneel, but others never kneel. Is it wrong to kneel? I say not. I can't kneel anymore since I had knee replacement surgery, but I must not be critical of those who do kneel and no one should be critical of me because I cannot kneel. Bowing or kneeling in worship, we declare that God and God alone is worthy of our worship. The Bible says that Jehosaphat bowed with his face to the ground. In Ephesians 3:14, Paul says, "For this cause I bow my knees to the Father of our Lord Jesus Christ." There are many places in Scripture where bowing or kneeling is mentioned. So it is okay to bow or kneel in worship of our living God.

Hand Clapping

"O Clap your hands all ye people; shout unto God with the voice of triumph."-Psalms 47:1. Isaiah 55:12 described the happiness of believers in Christ saying, "For ye shall go out with joy, and be led forth with peace: the mountains and the hills shall break forth before you into singing, and all the trees of the field shall clap their hands." Hand clapping can be a worship experience; however, applauding man and his performance is not worshipping God. Sometimes, people clap their hands in rhythm with the music. That can be worship, but many times it is entertainment. My grandmother, who was a very godly person, used to get happy and shout. In doing so, she would clap her hands. That, of course, is different from applauding or keeping time with the music. If hand clapping is done to bring glory and honor to God, then it is a part of the worship experience.

DANCING

"Let them praise His name in the dance: let them sing praises unto Him with the timbrel and harp."-Psalms 149:3. David danced before the Lord. I have seen people get so happy in the Lord that they danced as they praised the Lord. Although dancing is not my way of expressing praise and honor to God, it does not give me a right to be critical of those who dance in worship.

KNEELING

I have already mentioned kneeling with bowing but I would like to say at this point that kneeling is an act of reverence, as one would kneel in the presence of royalty. "Oh come, let us worship and bow down: let us kneel before the Lord our maker."-Psalms 95:6. "Now when Daniel knew that the writing was signed, he went into his house; and his windows being open in his chamber toward Jerusalem, he kneeled upon his knees three times a day, and prayed, and gave thanks before his God as he did aforetime."-Daniel 6:10. Many times in my life, it has seemed to me the right thing to do is to kneel before God. My two boys, Tony and Dan, heard me say that I would like to go to the World War II Memorial in Washington, D. C. They started making plans to take me there. The day was set and all was arranged for the venture. We flew out of Atlanta, Georgia to Washington, spent the night, and visited the beautiful memorial, and we visited a lot of other places. As I was walking around viewing all of the memorial displays of the War, I came by the one of the Normandy Invasion of which I was a part. I removed my cap, stood for a while, and then I went down on my knees and thanked God for all the thousands who gave their lives for our freedom. I thanked Him for bringing me home and giving me life and strength to be there. When I finished my prayer, standing up, I saw many people around me with their hats removed, standing in reverence. What a tremendous experience of the presence of God. It is pleasing to God to kneel before Him in deep, heart-felt, worship.

Leaping

A spontaneous act of joy, "Rejoice ye in that day, and leap for joy for behold your reward is great in Heaven: for in the like manner did their fathers unto the prophets."-Luke 6:23. The story in the Book of Acts of Peter and John going up to the temple to pray and encountering a lame man who was healed had a reaction of leaping. "And leaping he stood up and walked and entered with them into the temple, walking, and leaping, and praising God."-Acts 3:8.

Lifting Hands

"Let my prayer be set forth before thee as incense; and the lifting up of my hands as the evening sacrifice."-Psalms 141:2. "I will therefore that men pray everywhere, lifting up holy hands without wrath and doubting."-I Timothy 2:8. Lifting of hands is associated with the act of surrender. When one lifts their hands in worship, they are saying to God, "I surrender my whole being to You." It is also an act of pleading. A child lifts its hands saying, "Take me, pick me up." Many years ago now, our family had gathered at our house during the Thanksgiving holiday. My wife said to me, "I am out of potatoes. I got ready to go get some potatoes. We had plenty stored at the barn. I began getting my coat and hat on and secured a vessel to put the potatoes in. Our Granddaughter, Natalie, was very small. She was watching every move that I made, getting her coat and her toboggan on and said, "I am going too, Grandpa." I said, "You can't go, Nat. It is wet and muddy out there. You will get your feet muddy." She lifted up her little hands, looking into my face with those pleading eyes, and said, "You can carry me, Grandpa." Of course, everyone knows what I did. Many times, I have lifted up my spiritual hands and said to my Heavenly Father, "Pick me up. I just can't make it." He has always helped me over the tough places. When we lift up our hands of flesh to God, we must do it in reverence of Him as we surrender to Him and ask for help.

Shouting

"O clap your hands, all ye people; shout unto God with the voice of triumph."-Psalms 47:1. "Sing, O daughter of Zion; shout, O Israel; be glad and rejoice with all the heart, O daughter of Jerusalem."-Zephaniah 3:14. Shouting is an expression of joy and gladness. People jump, clap their hands, and yell when they win money on game shows or at ball games, but seldom do people express joy in like manner for the good blessings of our God. The question is, "Which is better?"

PLAYING MUSICAL INSTRUMENTS

"Praise Him with the sound of the trumpet: praise Him with psaltery and harp. Praise Him with the timbrel, and dance: praise Him with stringed instruments and organs. Praise Him upon the loud sounding cymbals: praise Him upon the high-sounding cymbals."-Psalms 150:3-5. This is to be done to bring glory to God and not for entertainment of man.

SINGING

"O come, let us sing unto the Lord: let us make a joyful noise to the rock of our salvation. Let us come before His presence with thanksgiving, and make a joyful noise unto Him with psalms."-Psalms 95:1-2. The secret of worshipping God in song is to sing unto the Lord. All too many times, Gospel singing is used to entertain man. This would be singing unto man instead of singing unto God. Thank God for people who use their God-given ability to bless the rest of us by singing unto the Lord.

STANDING

"And all the people saw the cloudy pillar stand at the tabernacle door: and all the people rose up and worshipped every man in his tent door."-Exodus 33:10. "And the Levites, of the children of the Kohathites, and of the children of the Korhites, stood up to praise the Lord God of Israel with a loud voice on high."-II Chron. 20:19. Standing is an act of honor and praise, as giving someone a standing ovation. We should stand in awe of the eternal God.

OFFERING

"Give unto the Lord the glory due unto His name: bring an offering, and come into His courts."-Psalms 96:8. Many places in the Scriptures, we are admonished to bring an offering to the Lord. This should always be an act of worship. It is not a collection, but an offering unto the Lord. It is a vital part of our corporate worship.

SILENCE

"But the Lord is in His holy temple: let all the earth keep silence before Him."-Habakkuk 2:20. "Be still, and know that I am God: I will be exalted among the heathen, I will be exalted in the earth."-Psalms 46:10. It is good to worship God quietly. Sometimes we need to just get still and be quiet and let God speak to our hearts.

In worship, we get what we seek for; a nice comfortable service or we can leave with the wonder of having stood in the presence of the Pilot, Himself. My heart has been changed and my life challenged by this study.

I endeavored to try to visit every church in the Association every year while I was the Association Missionary. This was almost an impossible task, but it was a challenge and a great blessing. The people always welcomed me with open arms. I experienced a variety of worship styles and found myself enjoying the presence of God among His people. Doors of opportunity were opened to me that would have never been mine had it not been for the God-given opportunity to serve in this position.

I kept a record of the churches I visited and tried to visit those I hadn't been to recently. If I didn't have an appointment on a Sunday morning or Sunday night, I would pray to God asking Him for guidance as to where He wanted me to go. It always proved out that when I arrived at my destination, there was a needed ministry waiting for me. One Sunday, I had been earnestly praying concerning where God wanted me to go. When I started out that morning, I followed His directions. It was a cold winter morning. With some light snow blowing, when I arrived, I noticed there were only two cars in the parking lot. I went in and found two ladies and three children hovered around a gas, floor furnace trying to keep warm. One of the ladies, while brushing tears from her cheeks, looked at me and said, "I know God sent you here this morning." I said, "You are right. God did indeed send me here." I asked about their Pastor and she said, "He is gone. We don't have anyone to lead us." I taught the Sunday School lesson for them and prayed with them. I then brought a brief message of encouragement. "God will never leave us or forsake us." I couldn't go back the next Sunday. I already had an appointment, but two weeks later, I went back and we had sixteen present. Two precious children accepted the Lord as their Savior that morning. God blessed me with the privilege of helping them to get back on track and call a Pastor. Now, more than forty years later, they are still growing strong. "Well glory!" This is just one example of many things that occurred during my twenty-six years of tenure as Director of Missions in the mountains of Western, North Carolina.

In January of 1965, I went to Macedonia (Wolf Creek) Church at the invitation of the Pastor to teach January Bible Study. It has been a practice for many years that the Southern Baptist Convention publishes a study course book on one of the books of the Bible for January Bible Study. I started doing this when I was pastor of Little Brasstown Baptist Church and liked the practice. When I arrived at Wolf Creek Baptist Church on Sunday night through Wednesday, I discovered there were some people present from neighboring churches. It went real well with good attendance and a lot of excitement.

The next year, three of the churches nearby wanted me to come to their church and teach the study also. I couldn't do that for I had already scheduled some work in other churches during January and February. I suggested that the four churches in close proximity come together at one location for the study. They readily agreed to do so. Macedonia, Hopewell, Mt. Moriah, and Simonds Chapel Baptist Church were the participants. I kept doing this year after year. When I retired as Association Missionary in 1990, they wanted me to keep on teaching them. This year will be forty-four years of having the wonderful blessing of sharing the Word of God with these precious people. Most of the people that started with me forty-four years ago are already gone on to be with the Lord while younger ones have taken their places. To God be the glory for all the wonderful blessings that He has given me along the way.

As I have already indicated, Rev. Willard Graham took the leadership of the West Liberty Association in 1965. We worked together with a great relationship, but he came to me and said he was going to retire from the association work in 1970. He said the West Liberty Association wanted me to take it back and do both associations as before. I told him the only way I would do that was if they would look with favor of merging the two associations into one. This way we could have the strength to do more and greater ministries. They voted to do that and he agreed to help me put it all together. In 1969, the two associations met together and voted to merge and drop both names and the Association was named The Truett Baptist Association in honor of the family of Dr. George W. Truett. He grew up in the area. In 1970, we had the First Annual Session of the Truett Baptist Association.

From early childhood days, I always had a heart for Sunday School. We only had preaching one Sunday each month but we had Sunday School every Sunday. I thank God for the godly people, mostly women, who cared enough about us children to teach us the Bible. Before I answered the call to preach, I served as Sunday School Superintendent and Teacher. When I became a Pastor, Sunday School was always a priority. In the early days of my working in Association Mission work, the Sunday School Board of the Southern Baptist Convention asked me to go to Nashville, Tenn. for training to become a leader in the Sunday School Growth Campaign Movement in the 1960's. My first assignment was in Haywood Baptist Association at Waynesville, N. C. I was assigned one church and was to stay with them all week long, teaching them and helping them set up an Outreach Ministry and a Teaching Plan for their church. It proved to be a great blessing with the church growing by reaching and teaching new people through their Reaching, Teaching Plan. After that initial experience, I was privileged to do many of these events over the next twenty years or so. When I retired in 1990, I moved right into Sunday School work in the decade of the 90's, which I will mention later.

The Utah Experience

Every year, the Baptist Home Mission Board held what they called Home Mission Week at Ridgecrest, the National Baptist Assembly Ground at Black Mountain, N. C. I went every year to this very important event of training, inspiration, and challenge. I had the God-given opportunity to help lead a variety of conferences for several years. One year in the late 1970's, this meeting was of a very high spiritual nature. God moved on our hearts in a very special way. One of our speakers who was a Baptist Missions Leader, challenged us to volunteer to go somewhere in the United States to a Pioneer Missions Area to preach a revival at our own expense. When the invitation was given, I went forward, saying I would step out on faith to do just that. Dr. Jim Smith spoke about the great need for a revival effort in Chicago. I decided this was the place for me and turned my name in as a volunteer for the Simultaneous Revival Effort in 1979. I was having some second thoughts about all of this as time passed. It was a big thing. Where would I get the money? I was all the while praying about the whole thing.

On Wednesday night, I went to prayer meeting at Mount Carmel Baptist Church in the Hiawassee Dam Community. During the course of the service, the pastor asked for people to give prayer requests. I got up and asked them to join me in praying about this mission trip. At the close of the service, a sweet little old lady came to me in the church parking lot and handed me a twenty-dollar bill and said, "When you go on this trip for our Lord, buy yourself some hamburgers." I thanked her and got in my car and started toward home, praying as I drove. After driving a few miles, I stopped beside the road, got out and looked up into the star-studded sky, thanking God for all of His wonder. I reached in my pocket and took out the twenty-dollar bill saying to Him, "This belongs to you. What would you have me do with it?" In His still small voice, He spoke to my heart using the words of the little woman, "Buy yourself some hamburgers when you go. I have plenty more. I own the cattle of a thousand hills, the silver and the gold." I went down on my knees in the grass and fully committed myself to Him to go at His command. A few days later, I received a call from Ken Carter who worked in Evangelism with the Home Mission Board in Atlanta, Ga. He said, "Fred, I have a place for you to go during this National Simultaneous Revival Effort. I want you to go to Utah." I said, "Ken, I have already told Jim Smith that I would go to Chicago." He replied, "I have talked to Jim since you have. I want you to enlist three other preachers and a couple of laymen to go with you. I will give you the details later." I didn't want to go to Utah. It was too far from home, besides it was Morman country. Very little Baptist work existed in the States of Utah and Idaho. Just a few days later my friend, Richard Powers said to me, "I know where you ought to go on your mission trip." I replied, "Where?" He said, "We went on vacation last year out West and visited Salt Lake City, Utah. That's where you need to go." To say the least, I almost fainted. He didn't know a thing about my call from Ken Carter. I began praying about whom should go and how God would have us to put it all together. It ended up that three Pastors agreed to go. All three of them were fine dedicated men of God. Chester Jones, Buddy Pittman, and Harold Miller were their names. Francis Cook, a layman, went to work with Buddy Pittman and Rex Ware, a young nineteen year old, went to help me. He was a good piano player and singer. He was enlisted to fill the need in the church where I was assigned. Chester, Harold, Rex, and myself were all located in the Salt Lake City, Utah area, while Buddy and Francis were assigned to a church about three hundred miles North in Idaho.

We left Marble Springs Baptist Church on Tuesday evening, April 10, 1979. We were traveling in a motor home loaned to us by Frank Rose, Jr. and a car belonging to Francis Cook. The motor home hadn't been driven for a while, so, late Tuesday night, the filter on the gas line stopped up. We had to stop and replace the filter before proceeding on our journey.

We strapped our luggage on top of the motor home on the luggage rack. While traveling on the interstate in Louisiana, I was riding in the car behind the motor home. I saw a suitcase rise up on its end on top of the motor home. The wind caught it and here it came, hitting the highway, bouncing a time or two, and ended up on the centerline of the highway. We stopped, picked it up, put it in the trunk of the car. Sure enough, it was mine. It was broken all to pieces. Luckily, I had put it in a plastic garbage bag to keep it dry. We had C. B. Radios in both vehicles to keep in contact with each other as we traveled, but that bunch in the motor home had theirs turned off. We finally caught up with them and did a better job securing the luggage. I bought me a new suitcase when we stopped on the rim of the Grand Canyon.

A big storm occurred in West, Texas, producing a strong head wind as we traveled across the State. It was necessary to stop at most gas stations to gas up. I think we got about five miles per gallon.

One night late, we were traveling along making good time. Harold Miller was driving the motor home. I was riding shotgun and Chester and Rex were in the back asleep. The dining table folded up and made a bed. The table leaf was supporting the mattress. We heard a great commotion and turned on the light. Chester and Rex both were lying in the floor. Chester had his hand over his mouth and nose with blood dripping out between his fingers. Harold got off the road as quickly as he could so we could assess the situation. We were gaining altitude and Chester had developed a nosebleed in his sleep. He awoke, capped his hand over his nose and put his feet out of the bed rather quickly, putting his whole three-hundred pound weight on the table leaf and broke it slap in two, thus, dumping him and Rex both in the floor. When we arrived in Utah, Chester got a new table leaf made which was much stronger than the original one.

We stopped in Fort Worth, Texas to have lunch with Harold Millers' daughter and her husband. He was a student in Southwestern Seminary, and then we continued on our journey into New Mexico. We stopped in Flag Staff, Arizona on Thursday, April 12. I said, "Fellows, we have the money so let's get a motel room and spend the night. I am completely given out." People had been very generous, giving us money and food for the trip and we had plenty.

I went to bed and soon went to sleep. I woke up the next morning, put my feet on the floor just as tired as I was when I went to bed. I was the oldest one in the crowd, so I tired quickly and rested slowly. We got a good, hot, shower, ate breakfast, and then headed toward Utah, stopping on the rim of the Grand Canyon. We boiled hot dogs for lunch. They liked to have never boiled at that high altitude. We got into Utah that night, got a motel room again, and on Saturday morning, we traveled on into Salt Lake City, Utah by 12:00 noon. People from the churches where we were to work met us at First Southern Baptist Church of Salt Lake to take us where we would be staying. Buddy and Francis traveled another three hundred miles into Idaho. Rex and I went to stay at the home of some people, who operated an Arabian Horse Farm, raising and training show horses.

The next day was Easter Sunday morning, April 15. We were to be in First Baptist Church of West Jordan, Utah. It was in Salt Lake City proper. The Executive Secretary of the Utah, Idaho Convention had called me telling me that there was not much prospect for revival in that church. They had only eighteen members consisting of one adult male member and the rest were women and children. They had no pastor and hadn't had a revival in four years. They were meeting in the basement of an old house. Rex was to be in charge of the music on Sunday morning. As a result of this responsibility, he was really uptight, asking me what we were going to do. I told him, "I am very tired and I don't know what we will do, but I am trusting the Lord for that, therefore, I am going to bed and going to sleep and I suggest that you do the same."

A strange thing happened. I got a good nights' rest, waking up the next morning feeling rested and so fresh and good. I was ready to go for the Lord.

I stood up to preach that morning in a whole different setting, but the very same God that always was with me in North Carolina was with me there.

A lady in the church who had two cars gave us a car to drive the whole week. We visited people every day and had services every night. Sometimes, the services lasted late at night. We had services all week long and finished up the following Sunday morning. When we started, they had eighteen members, but when we finished, they had thirty-six members. They doubled in one week. What a wonderful blessing God had lavished on us. The other three men also had great results; however, West Jordan had more additions than any other church in the entire Utah, Idaho Convention.

The church owned a plot of ground and had some money in hand to build a church. They had employed an architect but he was dragging his feet, failing to help them get a building permit. I met with him and told him that his architect license could be in jeopardy if he was taking their money and not getting them a building permit. Maybe my little talk helped, because they had a building permit in about a month.

They poured the slab for the building. A group of Baptist men from Texas went and dried it in for them. One year later, I went back and preached another revival in the new building. When I left that time, they had seventy-two members instead of the thirty-six the year before. Thank God for His mighty power and for allowing me to be a small part of His work.

We left Salt Lake City on Sunday afternoon, April 22, heading back home. We got a motel room and rested Sunday night after traveling some distance then we drove straight through. We stopped in the Rabbit Ear Pass in Colorado and had a prayer meeting in Colorado. The snow was very deep.

Many funny things happened along the way. Time or space will not allow me to share all of them, but I will share one more experience. Since we had gone the Southern route out there, we came back the Northern route. We stopped for breakfast and got gas in Kentucky. Harold was driving and Chester was in the back asleep. He pulled into a gas station and was pumping gas. He had on a little pair of tennis shoes to drive in. Chester came out about half asleep and stepped on Harold's foot. Harold just fell back, grabbed his foot, jerked off his shoe and sock and said, "You have mashed my toe off." Sure enough, he had a toe missing. Chester stood there in awe. However, Harold's toe had been missing for many years, but Chester didn't know that. What a great bunch. None of our lives have been the same since we had those two weeks together in the awesome work of our Lord.

YOUTH ON MISSION FOR CHRIST

One of the outstanding things that took place during my tenure, as Director of Missions, was the opportunity of working with the young people of the two-county area. We had a Youth Council made up of young people from different churches with a Pastor as Pastor Advisor. They elected a Youth Director and an Assistant. One Sunday afternoon each month, we had a Youth Prayer Meeting in one of the churches. A youth choir was organized with a Director to practice and sing at various events.

Several years, the youth sponsored an Association Youth Revival, bringing in an outside speaker. Most of our churches were small and could not have a Youth Minister or Director. This Youth on Mission for Christ Organization gave all the young people an opportunity to be involved in something constructive for Christ. All of those young people who were in the Youth on Mission for Christ Organization are now adults. Some of them have grown children of their own.

I still have feed back from many of those people, telling me what a blessing those days were to them and how it helped them to make right decisions for life.

The last person to serve as Youth Director for the Youth on Mission Organization is the same person who is now helping me to put this book together. She is none other than Sharon Kephart.

I left the Association work at the end of March 1990 at age sixty-five. If I had stayed fifty days longer, I would have served in this position for twenty-six years.

Following, is an excerpt of a news article that appeared in Home Mission Magazine in 1988:

In the Appalachian Mountains, West of Asheville, N. C., Fred Lunsford has devoted most of his life to serving God and His people. A native of Marble, N. C., Lunsford pastored a church in the area for 14 years before becoming Director of Missions for the Truett Baptist Association in 1964. Working closely with the people of this area has given him a special sensitivity and insight into their needs as well as an understanding of the mountainous area.

Truett Baptist Association has the highest number of bi-vocational churches of any North Carolina association. Of the 64 churches in the association, 45 have bi-vocational pastors. Many of these churches lack the personnel for extensive progress, and the association is able to fill in some of the gaps. Lunsford leads his association to develop many special ministries that have traditionally begun in a local church. For instance, a youth organization begun in 1971 helps young people in an association of small country churches find activities and direction in a Christian setting. The association also leads in a ministry called People First, which is aimed at handicapped individuals. This six-year-old ministry sponsors retreats as well as educational programs for its specific target group.

A volunteer-run ministry to the blind is also an integral part of Lunsford's association. Furnishing tapes and tape players to visually impaired people is only part of this active service. The ministry also provides special assistance and helps to individuals in whatever ways their needs dictate. An association deaf ministry provides many of the same features with the addition of sign language classes. Many local churches participate by having meetings in their facilities, but Lunsford's primary goal is to reach people in need.

The Truett Baptist Association is located in the Southwest corner of North Carolina. This beautiful region of Appalachia is witnessing many changes, and Lunsford is preparing his association for opportunities resulting from these changes. These changing situations in the association call for long-range planning in order to meet anticipated needs.

Lunsford asserts that the basic needs of people everywhere are the same. The large number of bi-vocational pastors calls for leadership training. Following the call of God, many pastors' go to churches that are unable to fully support them. To help meet the bi-vocational pastor's needs, Lunsford speaks proudly of the Seminary Extension Program in the association, which he says is "second to none." Since the Seminary Extension Program began in 1951, there has been a center in the Truett Association. Many pastors, especially bi-vocational pastors, are involved in the extension program. Lunsford has excellent qualifications to lead an association with such a high number of bi-vocational pastors. He started out as a bi-vocational pastor and has worked his way through the

Seminary Extension Program. His example shows many young pastors options and choices available to them.

Lunsford enjoys hunting and fishing in the region where he grew up. His garden takes some of his time and he says his wife, Gladys, prefers flower gardens. Still, his greatest pleasure comes from his work—the Lord's work. Many people ask him why he does not take more time off, but Lunsford's reply is simple: He loves doing what he is called to do; he loves his mission.

When Lunsford considers some of the Bible verses that have helped him in his 24 years as Director of Missions, he says that his personal favorite must be the second part of Matthew 28:20. Jesus' assurance that He is with us always, even to the end of the world, gives security and strength, says Lunsford. Other favorites include Psalm 100:2 and some very practical applications in James. But the driving principle of Lunsford's association work is found in I Corinthians 3:9. There, Paul speaks of being laborers together with God. Lunsford sees that as the basic ideal of the association and church; helping churches and working with God to win people.

In 1987, Lunsford received the Home Mission Board award for outstanding leadership in an eastern rural-urban association. While presenting this award, Robert Wiley, Director of the Home Mission Board's Associational Missions Division, asked Lunsford how he had managed to get so much done in his association. When Lunsford started his work, he even ran the association from the trunk of a car! Lunsford explained that when he was starting out, he decided to keep bees. He acquired a hive and set it up in the backyard. Using the hive as a base for their work, soon the bees produced honey.

People also need a base from which to work, Lunsford asserts. The people in Truett Association are busy as they help in association work, and Lunsford is quick to give them credit for all they do. He quickly emphasizes, however, that the praise and glory go to God. "Developing communication, teamwork, love, and acceptance are the main principles I work with," states this very special Director of Mission, Fred Lunsford.

One of the great things I had an opportunity to do during those twenty-six years was to do the work of an evangelist. I did a lot of witness training events, preached many church revivals, and area wide crusades. I will attempt to share a few of these experiences from these times.

RETIRED, RECYCLED

At age sixty-five, a big change was made in my life. I couldn't say that I was retired, but more like recycled. The first four or five months after retiring from the mission work, I served as Interim Pastor for Macedonia Baptist Church, located on Wolf Creek near the Tennessee line. We had a very enjoyable time with the fine people of this wonderful church. I would go to the community on Wednesday mornings and do some visiting, and then I would be there for the midweek Prayer Meeting. The church was blessed with some elderly ladies that were widows. When I arrived in the community, I would stop by for a pastoral visit with one of them. By the time I got to the next one, they all knew I was in the community. Consequently, they were on the lookout for me and would have the coffee made to go with their very delicious goodies. God blessed greatly during those very enjoyable days of ministry.

During those months, Mr. Robert Stewart and Mr. Maurice Cooper contacted me. They were on the staff of the North Carolina Baptist State Convention. They contacted me in regards to the possibility of becoming a Church Growth Consultant for the Convention. They were putting together what was called a team of "Church Growth Multipliers." The work was to major on church growth through church programs such as Sunday School, Discipleship Training, Brotherhood, and Woman's Missionary Union.

I agreed to the assignment after much prayerful consideration. They divided the State into three sections, the East, the Piedmont, and the West. I was made Team Leader for the Western part of the State. This territory covered from Statesville all the way to Western North Carolina. Maurice Cooper was our Supervisor so he was the one who enlisted the team members. The Western Team was made up of two men and five women. They were: James Clouse from Hendersonville, Martha Hicks of Asheville, Helen Alan of Ridgecrest, Suthel Walker of Forest City, Mabel Couch of Wilksboro, and Sharon Kephart of Murphy. While doing the work, Robert Stewart, as head of the Sunday School work, asked me to put together a Church Growth Plan through the Sunday School. We called it a "Sunday School Growth Revival." This approach was put into place in 1991. During the decade of the nineties, I was privileged to be in about one hundred and fifty churches in North Carolina, as well as some in Tennessee, South Carolina, Alabama, Georgia, and in West Virginia doing this work. Sharon Kephart became a specialist in Outreach and Care Ministry in Sunday School in order to help with the effort, as well as doing a lot with Woman's Missionary Union.

This work began to slow down some in 1997, therefore, freeing me up to some other things. However, these ten years of ministry were a tremendous blessing to me. Many people were a great help to me in order to make this effort a great success story. Maurice Cooper is now gone on to be with the Lord. Robert Stewart is retired, but continues to be quite busy in Sunday School work across the State. One of my team members has now gone on to his reward. He was Jim Clouse and I know he had a great reward awaiting him in glory, because he was a great Christian leader up until his departure. I thank God for all of these wonderful people.

To close out this chapter in my story, I will share a very interesting incident that I will always remember. Periodically, our Church Growth Multiplier Team had to go to the Baptist Building in Cary, North Carolina for training and evaluation. Jim Clouse, Mabel Couch, and Suthel Walker decided to go on their own, but the rest of us car pooled. Sharon Kephart drove her car from Murphy to Ridgecrest and parked her car at Helen Alan's house at Ridgecrest, North Carolina. I picked up Martha Hicks at her house in West Asheville and then picked up Sharon and Helen at Ridgecrest. We had a good trip going down to the meeting. We stayed two days and nights. The day we were to leave, they told us they were going to let us go a bit early because the weather forecast was calling for snow. Suthel Walker was staying over for another meeting and Mr. Clouse left before we did. As the three ladies and myself were going down the road, the ladies decided they would like to stop and eat at a Cracker Barrel Restaurant. We stopped at Burlington, parked, and went in the Cracker Barrel Restaurant. It was just beginning to snow flurry a bit. We ate a good lunch, paid our bill, went to the restrooms, and came out to get on our way. It was snowing some of the largest snowflakes I had ever seen. The ground was already white. Traveling I-40 West, it looked plenty dark up ahead. Traffic was beginning to slow and some cars were spinning out and crashing here and there. Martha Hicks would look out the window and say, "Lordie, Lordie, Lordie." She did that several times and Helen Alan said, "Martha, I wish you would hush that 'Lordie' business." Martha didn't pay any attention and she continued saying it again and again, and we all had a good laugh.

We discussed the possibility of getting rooms and spending the night at Winston-Salem, but after prayerful consideration, we decided to go on our way. The snow got deeper as we traveled West. We arrived at Ridgecrest all safe and sound. When we raked the snow off of Sharon's car, it was four inches deep. She finally got out of Helen's driveway and followed me to Martha's house in West Asheville. Martha tried to get us to spend the night with her, but I needed to get home. I had told my wife that I would be home about 7:00 p. m. We left Asheville with Sharon following me. The snow kept piling up on I-40. We got just West of the Canton/Candler Exit and the traffic stopped dead. We were still bumper-to-bumper and nobody was moving westbound. A State Trooper came along in the eastbound lanes and stopped. I asked him what the problem was. He said a tractor-trailer rig had jack-knifed about three miles ahead. They were having trouble getting wreckers to the site. I asked him about the roads heading West. He asked me where I was headed and I told him I was going to Murphy. He said, "You won't be going tonight, because the road is closed through the Nantahala Gorge." I asked him about US 64 through Franklin, North Carolina. He said it was closed also. I thought, "What am I going to do?" Gladys, my wife, was expecting me home by 7:00. It was now 5:30 and under normal conditions we were about two hours away. Sharon had a cell phone, but I did not. I got out of my car; the snow was falling so hard I could hardly see. I went back to her car and told her the situation. I said, "Can you get out on your phone?" She said she could do so. I said to her, "You better call your mom and dad and tell them that you won't be home until tomorrow sometime. Then, let me borrow your phone and call my wife, Gladys." Sharon said, "Where are we going to stay?" I said, "I don't know, but if you can get the phone number of the Days Inn Motel at the exit we just passed, I suggest that you call them and ask them to hold us two rooms for the night." She did this. The traffic began to move about 9:00 p. m. We went to the next exit, crossed over, and went East to the Canton/Candler Exit where the motel was located. Snow was picking up and the temperature was dropping. Cars were off the road everywhere. We checked in the motel. Sharon called her dad and mom and I called Gladys. Robert Stewart had called my wife to see where we were. My son, Dan, who lived at Hillsboro, called also. They had all heard about the snowstorm. Gladys gave them the number of the motel and they all called me. Dan said, "Dad, one thing you are going to do is get a cell phone." So I did just that.

The next morning was Sunday morning. I got up and looked out. Snow was banked up because the wind had howled all night long and it was still snowing at seventeen degrees. My car was parked alongside of Sharon's car on the West side. Snow had drifted up against the right side of it up to the windows.

They called from the motel office, which was at the bottom of the hill and told us they had bought some breakfast cereal and milk for people staying in the motel. A great number of the people staying there were snow bound from several different states.

The only shoes I had were dress, ventilated, slippers. I got a couple of grocery bags I had in the car and put them on over my shoes, tying the tops on my legs to wade the snow down to the office. I brought some breakfast back to Sharon for her to eat in her room.

The temperature came up very little that day. I called the State Trooper's Office to find out about the roads, although, I had seen the report on the television. It looked like all roads were impassable. They informed me that I could not get home before Monday. I had plenty of time to pray, read God's Word, and reflect.

Monday afternoon, we got on our way home with one lane of the road being cleared going West and one lane was cleared going East. The Nantahala Gorge was still closed so we traveled US 64 through Franklin, North Carolina. The report was that there were eighteen inches of snow at Waynesville. There was more in some other places. At my home, there was around six inches. Thank God for His tender care extended to all of us by His marvelous grace. "Well glory!"

Robbinsville Experience

In October of 1997, I received a telephone call from Jack Lovin, a Deacon in First Baptist Church, Robbinsville, N. C. He asked me if I could come and preach for them on November 9. I was glad to go and help them because I had preached in that church many times over the years and I learned to love them. While there, they informed me that they were out of a pastor and asked me if I would come and preach some for them. I helped them in November and December. January was booked up with Bible studies and Sunday School Conferences for me. In February, I started helping them on a regular basis and they elected me as their Interim Pastor. I told them not to consider me as their full-time pastor because I felt I was too old. They needed more than I had to offer. Good things started happening, people were being saved, and the church was growing.

The Pastor Search Committee had been working for some time, looking at several preachers. They had heard some of them preach and also interviewed them. On a given Sunday morning, they told me they wanted to talk to me that night. I agreed to talk with them. I was thinking they just needed some advice. All the while, I had firmly made up my mind that I would not become their pastor. My wife and I were living in the parsonage part-time, still maintaining our home at Marble, N. C. which was twenty-eight miles away. It was getting close to time for the Sunday night service. I had just finished eating a sandwich and a knock came at the back door. I went to the door and there stood my long time friend and fellow preacher, Rev. Frank James. He was a member of the church, but was not physically able to attend. He said, "The Lord sent me over here to tell you something. I heard you preach on the radio this morning and God really blessed me through your message. God told me to come and tell you that He has you where He wants you and you better stay with it." I said, "Are you sure?" He replied, looking right in my eyes and said, "When God tells me something, I am sure that I am sure. You better listen." He then prayed a prayer and left.

When I met with the Committee, they told me that they had considered several people for their pastor, but God closed all the doors. They said they were all in agreement that I was to be their pastor. They knew I had told them not to consider me but they said that God told them differently. I then told them about Franks' visit. I also told them that I had decided to say, "No," but I now know that it is God's will for me to stay if I get a good healthy vote from the church. The vote was taken three weeks later. It was eighty-nine votes for me and two against me. Although I was seventy-three years old, I had three and one-half wonderful years with the good people of Graham County. I saw the church grow numerically and spiritually.

Early on in my ministry with these good people of First Baptist Church, I began to get a heavy burden for Graham County. I would go to the church on Saturday night all by myself and kneel in the altar without turning on the lights and I would have time alone with the Lord. On one of these very good occasions while I was praying, God moved on my heart to call some of the pastors in the county and invite them to breakfast at one of the restaurants in town. When I called, they were surprised that I would do that. Several came for the free breakfast. We ate and talked after a time of prayer. When we had finished eating, I told them about my burden for Graham County and that I would like to have a day of prayer on a Saturday. They liked the idea. I asked where they wanted to go. Rev. Daniel Stewart, Pastor of Cedar Cliff Baptist Church, said, "Let's go to the Hooper Bald." We all agreed and set a date, agreeing to meet and eat breakfast at Phillips' Restaurant before going on up to the mountain. Five of us showed up. After breakfast, we went to Hooper Bald. That day I shall never forget because the idea for a Countywide Revival was birthed on the mountain that day.

We planned the revival to be held at First Baptist Church a few months hence. A Saturday Men's Prayer Breakfast was held at the church on a Saturday morning. The men of the church cooked the breakfast and what a breakfast we had. Ninety-five men from across the County came, but greatest of all, God came. All of us went away with full stomachs and hearts overflowing with the love of God. Everyone was talking about the great power of the Holy Spirit.

The revival services started on a Sunday night. The sanctuary was full, including the balcony. Chairs were brought in and some people were standing. They told us that people came that night and couldn't get inside. A different pastor preached each night and Ronnie Shuler led the singing. A wonderful outpouring of God's Spirit brought revival to all that attended. Fifteen churches from across the county participated. People still talk about this wonderful experience. Thank God for His goodness. I still have a burden for revival for Graham County as well as Cherokee County where I live.

I thank God for all the wonderful people of Robbinsville First Baptist Church and for all of Graham County, for that matter. I have preached in most all of the Baptist churches in the County and what a blessing it has been. I would like to call the names of people but if I did, I would miss someone and I don't want to do that.

Among many things that were accomplished, there was a vote to make Robbinsville First Baptist Church a "Lighthouse Church." In order to do that, people committed themselves to be "Lighthouse Christians."

When I left the church, I was praying, asking God what He wanted me to do. He spoke to my heart that I should start a Christian Lighthouse Ministry. I will discuss this briefly a bit later.

I prayed much about leaving the church. God showed me beyond the shadow of a doubt, that it was time for me to go. I really wanted to stay with the wonderful people, but God said, "It is time for you to go." I sat in the parking lot of the beautiful brick church building, which sits on a hill overlooking the town of Robbinsville, N. C. I had sat there before and prayed to God for Him to give me Robbinsville for His glory. The sun was setting in the West with beautiful gray and crimson clouds reflecting God's loving beauty. Tears streamed down my face. God said, "This is yours forever. Remember you have me."

Ministry at Vengeance Creek Baptist Church

"My thoughts are not your thoughts, neither are your ways my ways, saith the Lord. For as the heavens are higher than the earth, so are my ways higher than your ways, and my thoughts than your thoughts."-Isaiah 55:8-9.

"I have raised him up in righteousness, I will direct all his way."-Isaiah 45:15.

My residence has been on Vengeance Creek all of my life except for a few years when we lived in Murphy and Peachtree. However, my church membership has been in other churches most of the time. When I went to Robbinsville First Baptist Church in 1998, we moved our membership from Marble Springs Baptist Church to Robbinsville First Baptist Church. When we left Robbinsville, we prayed about what church we would move our membership to. We lived about half way between Marble Springs Baptist Church and Vengeance Creek Baptist Church. Of course, there were other churches nearby as well. I think most people assumed that we would move our membership back to Marble Springs since we were members there before. Since I wasn't pastoring anymore, we attended different churches and enjoyed it very much because we got to see old friends and had the privilege of worshipping with them.

After a few months, my wife said, "I think it is about time we get settled into a church and move our membership." I said, "I agree. We have jumped around like grasshoppers long enough. Where do you think we ought to go?" She said, "I have been praying about it and I think we ought to go to Vengeance Creek." I agreed readily because I had been praying also and I had the same feelings. I talked with the Pastor, Rev. Ronnie Palmer, about the possibility of us being members of his church. He said, "I would be delighted to have you and Gladys as members. I would like very much to be your Pastor." We joined the church in the spring of 2002. Fifty-six years had passed since we were members of our home church. We moved our membership when we moved to Pleasant Valley Baptist Church right after our first child was born. We both have family in the church. Gladys has a brother who is a Deacon and she also has nieces and their families. My sister, Furel, went on to be with the Lord a short while ago. My younger sister, Beatrice Rose and her husband, Kendal, also a Deacon of the church are members at Vengeance Creek. Beatrice has been involved in the music program of the church for many years serving as Music Director, playing the piano, and singing. Other members of her family are involved also.

A short while after I joined the church, the Pastor said to me, "I am glad you have joined the church. I am having some heart problems and I need to go have something done about it and when I do, I want you to take over for me and preach while I am out." I was involved with some other churches in the Christian Lighthouse Ministry but told him I would be glad to help out any way I could. Ronnie was a longtime friend of mine. He had been pastor of the church for twenty-seven years at that time. I had the distinct privilege of helping ordain him to the Gospel ministry when he began his ministry and Vengeance Creek Baptist Church and helped him in the church several times over the years. The church had grown under his ministry, building new buildings and adding new members week by week. The people at the church loved him with a passion. His wife, Barbara, is a very dedicated, radiant, Christian and helped him in the ministry. They have two children that grew up in the church, Derrick and Lisa.

Ronnie went into the hospital, had open-heart surgery, and was recovering quite well, but then he had some complications and he was never able to return to the pulpit as pastor. The church had prayer meetings at the church every night for a whole year. He continued to be the pastor that year and I filled the pulpit for him. At the end of one year, the doctor told him he would never be able to preach again. How sad this was. He took disability and resigned the church.

I was asked to be Interim Pastor. I told them I would do this, but I was not to be considered for full-time pastor because I was too old. After a few months, the Pastor Search Committee asked me to meet with them. They said that they had prayed and looked far and wide, but the only answer they could get from God was that I should stay as pastor. I found out again, as I have many times through the years, that God's ways are higher than my ways and I must follow God's ways and not mine. I agreed, after praying that I would stay on awhile until God told me it was enough. God really blessed by saving souls and using his people to minister for a total of about four years. During that time, Ronnie's son, Derrick, announced his call to preach and we ordained him. It was a true blessing for me to ordain father and son.

I felt that God had me at Vengeance Creek Baptist Church for the purpose of helping the church make transition in a time of crisis. It was a real crisis for the church since they had the same pastor for twenty-eight years. Most of the membership of the church he had baptized, since he was the only pastor they had ever known. I was with them all during Ronnie's sickness. It was a blessing to all of us that he was able to be at the church some of the time. On November 26, 2006 at the young age of fifty-nine, our beloved pastor, preacher, and singer went home to be with the Lord. His life was short, but full.

God said it was time for me to give up the pastorate. I was now in my eighties and my health was failing. I couldn't do the work that I knew a pastor ought to do. A few months after I resigned, the church elected Ronnie's son, Derrick, as Pastor. Now Ronnie has left behind his son as Pastor and his daughter, Lisa Frye as Choir Director. I am still part of the church, working in Sunday School while helping other churches through Christian Lighthouse Ministry.

I thank God that I am still going at age eighty-four. My goal is to win more at eighty-four. "Well glory!"

WORLD MISSIONS CONFERENCES AND REVIVALS

I had the opportunity of speaking in many World Missions Conferences. I would go to an Association along with several other missionaries. The host of the Missions Conference would always have Foreign Missionaries, State Missionaries, and Association Missionaries. I was used by the Home Mission Board and the State Convention to speak on their behalf, and I also represented Association Missions. I went to many different places across North Carolina. I also went to Georgia, Tennessee, South Carolina, and Alabama. Most of the time, I would end up speaking in ten different churches from Sunday morning through the following Sunday night. A lot of good was accomplished for missions and evangelism. Most every place I went, one or more of the churches I spoke in invited me back for a revival which always proved to be a great blessing.

One such situation was in Georgia. I was scheduled to speak in several churches in the Blue Ridge and Ellijay areas. Sometime after that I received a call wanting me to come to Ellijay and be the speaker for a Countywide Crusade at the Gilmer County High School Football Stadium. My calendar was clear the week they wanted, so I accepted the invitation. Another door was opened. On the Saturday before the crusade started on Sunday, they had a meeting of all the workers of the revival at the football stadium. I drove down Georgia Five Highway praying and thinking about this big event. I saw a poster nailed to a telephone pole by the side of the road. I pulled over and read the sign. It said, "County crusade. Come hear Evangelist, Fred Lunsford." Then in smaller print, it gave the name of the music director.

I felt proud that my name was in the limelight, but as I drove on down the road, I kept seeing more posters. The farther I went the more scared I got. By the time I arrived at Ellijay, I was shaking like a dry leaf on a White Oak Tree, blown by a cold winter wind. Old Georgia Five became Main Street through the small town of Ellijay, Georgia. I came around the curve onto the straightway of Main Street through town. A big banner was stretched across the street that read, "Victory In Jesus Crusade." Then my name was in small letters. I pulled over into a parking place and bowed my head on the steering wheel and said, "Thank you, Lord that it didn't say, Victory in Fred Lunsford Crusade." While I was parked there under the banner, my pride melted before the victorious Savior and Lord. I cried out to Him, "Lord, mold me and make me after Your will."

I went on to the meeting. Plans were made. All was set up for the platform to be at the fifty-yard line on the home side of the field. Backup plans were made in case it rained. If it rained, we would move to the school gymnasium. The extended forecast called for rain during the week, but we prayed for God to stay the rain so we could have the services uninterrupted. We had no rain all week. It rained other places in Georgia, North Carolina, and Tennessee, but not at Ellijay, Georgia. Our last service was on Sunday afternoon one week later. We had a great service with a beautiful sunshiny afternoon. The service ended about 4:30 p.m. I started home, and to my dismay, before I got to Blue Ridge, I met a great downpour of rain. I said, "Thank you, Lord." God is so good. Well glory! Many souls were saved and God's children were blessed, including this preacher. All glory must go to our awesome, eternal, God.

One day I received a phone call from Rev. John Newman, a Pastor in the Copper Basin Association of Ducktown, Tennessee. He told me that he and some of the men had met and prayed about an Association-wide Revival. They felt that God would have me come and preach a few nights. I told him I would be glad to do so if we could work out a time agreeable with them. The time and place was worked out with us starting on a Monday evening with plans to go through Saturday night. The place was agreed on by all. It would be held at Zion Hill Baptist Church in Turtletown, Tennessee, which is just a few miles from the North Carolina line.

Calvin Cook was secured to lead the singing and I was to do the preaching. My practice in those days was to meet with the young people for prayer thirty minutes before the starting time of the service. I met with the youth; John met with the men and the ladies in another room. The first night, I had seven teenagers. We prayed together and I asked them to invite all of the people they could the next day, keeping count of how many they invited. We would keep a tally to see who could invite the most. Before we left the room, I asked them if they would be willing to give themselves totally to the Lord so that they could be a way of revival in their church, county, and school. They agreed to do that as we made a circle while holding hands. God lavished his Holy Spirit upon us in that little prayer meeting. The next night, we had twelve and Wednesday night; we had a room full of youth and as the week went on the group continued to grow.

In the service, nothing much happened on Monday and Tuesday. Then on Wednesday night, one little red headed boy got saved and on Thursday night, thirteen people got saved and all of heaven came down.

The revival service continued over three weeks. One night, a man came with someone who had been there every night. The rain was really coming down. People were gathering in great numbers. One man said to his friend, "This couldn't be a Baptist meeting because nineteen drops of water will keep twenty Baptists away from church."

All we had to do was sing a little, preach a little, and get back out of the way and watch the Lord work. A newspaper reporter interviewed me for an article he wrote for the paper. Following, is an excerpt from that article:

About the recent associational-wide revival in Copper Basin Association, he says...In the more than 20 years I have been serving as a minister, with opportunities to preach revivals in several states and observe the work of the Holy Spirit in many areas, I have never experienced anything so great as this. God's movement in the hearts and lives of the people, especially the young people of this area will make a lasting impression on the entire area. The impact has spilled over into North Carolina and Georgia, as well as surrounding areas in Tennessee. This has been the high point in my Christian life as well as in my ministry. To the best of my knowledge, decisions for Christ ran over 350 with a great number of these being professions of faith. Several young people committed their lives to full-time Christian service. It was such a thrill to see the high school students carrying the message of the Lord Jesus Christ back into Copper Basin High School. An invitation came from the Student Council and Principal to speak to the school assembly. This is one of the most thrilling experiences I have ever known. About 110 of the high school students came to the front of the auditorium to stand with me saying that they had made a commitment to Christ during the revival. About 30 or 40 gave their testimony to the fact of the living Christ in their lives and the glorious experience they had with Christ during this revival. One teacher said, "This school is not the same place since this great thing has happened. Our students are showing love for one another as never before."

I feel that this is what is needed in many of our communities.. Nothing more. nothing less than revival from God.

The Stanley Association and the North Carolina Baptist State Convention jointly sponsored a Bible Conference in the Stanley Association. They asked me to be a part of that effort by teaching on the Holy Spirit in the book of Acts. It was held five nights, Monday through Friday. Rev. Roy Taylor was Pastor of Grace Baptist Church in Ablemarle, North Carolina, the location where the Bible Conference was held. The Lord really blessed during those days of sharing God's Word. Before I left, Brother Taylor asked me to come back and preach a revival for a week in about three months.

The revival started on Sunday night and went through the following Sunday morning. The building would seat seven hundred and fifty people and was full every night. The Music Director used the song, "Sweet, Sweet, Spirit" as the theme song. God really blessed him and the music.

We scheduled a youth night on Thursday evening. The music was great and the Spirit of God was really sweet that night. They had to bring in chairs in order to seat the people. Several college students were there from the University of North Carolina, Chapel Hill. When the message was over and the invitation was given, young people came from everywhere, kneeling in the altar and making commitments to the Lord. Some decisions were for salvation while others were rededicating their lives to the Lord. About 10:30 p.m., a big football player from Chapel Hill made his way up onto the platform and told me he wanted to say something. I gave him the microphone and he said, "I have never experienced anything like this. I hear much being said about the generation gap. If you young people love these adults, let them know." The service erupted when young people went all over the congregation hugging necks of adults and praising God.

We left the church that night and went home. I was staying in the Pastor's home. I was very tired and soon went to sleep. The Pastor couldn't sleep, so he got up and went back to the church to find the service was still going. Many of the young people were going into the city to teenage hangouts and bringing them back to the church and praying with them and winning them to faith in Christ.

What a great outpouring of the Holy Spirit we experienced that week.

The glorious blessings of God have been mine over the years, miles beyond anything I could ever think about deserving. I mention a few of the marvelous experiences I have enjoyed but they have not all been mountain-top experiences. I have walked through many valleys also when it looked like all was lost. I shall just mention one of these.

I was called to preach revival for a week in a small mountain church with the services beginning on Sunday and going through Saturday. I believed God would have me do so. We had good singing and fair preaching all week long but nothing happened. As far as I knew, no one made a decision for good. I walked away feeling like my efforts were wasted, although I knew that God had called us to be faithful and not necessarily successful. Several years later, I received a phone call early in the morning. A voice on the other end asked me what time I would be in my office. I told him I would be there about 8:30 a.m. He said, "I will meet you there. I need to talk to you." He told me his name but it was not a familiar name to me. I wondered what he wanted. I thought, perhaps, it was another one of those people with a hard-luck story seeking a handout. This happened quite often. I arrived at the office about 8:15 a.m. and found him already there waiting for me. Sure enough, to my knowledge, I had never seen the man before.

We went into the office, sat down, and right away he asked me a question while looking me in the eye with a look of desperation on his face. He said, "Do you remember preaching a revival at Mount Moriah Church about four years ago?" I thought for a moment and answered him that I did in fact remember it. He said, "So do I. I was there one night and your message touched my heart. My life was and is a terrible mess. I knew God was speaking to me through you, but while you were having a prayer of invitation time, I slipped out and haven't been back in church since. I have lived with that message tugging at my heart all these years. I am here today to ask you to help me to find my way to God." I shared with him the best I could. He asked God for forgiveness, putting his faith and trust in God for salvation. He rejoiced in his new life in Christ Jesus and went on his way, thanking God and me for helping him.

That experience taught me a great lesson. All God wants from us is that we be faithful to Him in all things and leave the results to Him. Many times, we think we have failed. God continues to work in the hearts of the people we have touched.

Some Memorable Experiences

Thank God for Memories

"He is not here but is risen: remember how He spake unto you when He was yet in Galilee." Luke 24:6

I am sitting on a log on the top of Buckhorn Mountain. I am experiencing something wonderful. This mountain is the dividing mountain between Peachtree Community and Vengeance Creek Community. Part of the rain that falls on this mountain will flow into Peachtree Creek and on into the Hiawassee River. Then part of it flows North into Vengeance Creek and then flows into Valley River. Then it will run into Hiawassee River and Valley River and they will run together at Murphy, N. C. Many times, Christian friends are clustered together as one. Then the time comes when they go their separate ways, but one day they will come back together in heaven forever. This is just like the raindrops that fall together on top of this mountain, then some of them flow South while others flow North, but then after miles of the journey, they come back together and flow into the beautiful Hiawassee Lake.

My reason for being here is a definite blessing from God. My nephew, Bruce Rose and his son, Brian have a contract to cut a boundary of timber on this mountain. My dear friends, Marvin Guffey and Jim Vaught are here working with them. When I found out that they were going to be working in this place, I asked Bruce if I could come and be with them one day. They were so very kind to bring me along today. I can hear the chain saws buzzing in a distance, the birds are singing, and the squirrels are chirping as the fresh, cool, mountain breeze blows on my face.

I am actually sitting in a low place in the mountain called the Buckhorn Gap. There was a time my grandfather, Will Rogers, owned this land. He died and my grandmother owned it for a time. About seventy-three years ago, my dad and my Uncle Dock Rogers cleared a plot of ground right where I am sitting and planted a patch of beans. We lived about two miles from here down the steep mountain on the headwaters of Vengeance Creek. We had a work mule that we brought up here pulling a sled. When harvest time came, we picked at least twelve bushels of beans. My mother pickled beans by the barrels and dried beans making what we called, "Leather Britches." As I look at this place, I can hardly believe all this about the bean patch because large Poplar Trees, some as much as three feet in diameter, are growing where beans once grew. These trees will now be harvested.

I have been here many times over the years, but not in the last thirty years. Another time that I was here is quite clear in my memory. When I was seventeen years old and still in high school, I came up here hunting. I knew I would be going to take part in World War II soon. I came up here hunting all by myself. I was right where I am now sitting and I heard a clap of thunder, then rain began to fall. I looked for a place of shelter. A large tree had fallen and lodged in another tree. The tree trunk was very large and a few feet up off of the ground. I crawled under the tree in the dry leaves and began to pray while the furious storm raged as if the elements were angry. I lay there in the dry leaves for a bed and prayed. I, in my simple child-like way, asked God to take care of me. He manifested Himself to me in a way that is indescribable. He assured me that all would be well with me now and in years to come.

Many times over the years when the storms of life were raging, including the war, I have, in my mind, come back to this place and received strength from it to go on and bring my focus back on God.

Now I am eighty-three years old and back at this spot, probably for the last time in body, but it still remains solid and steadfast in my heart and mind forever. I have many memories of places where I have met God in these mountains that are very precious to me. Thank God for memories even at eighty-three years of age.

What a surprise when I started walking along a logging road to go back to where my friends were working and looked out the road and I saw two men walking toward me. As they got a little closer, I discovered it was my dear friend and fellow Christian, Cecil Lovingood and his son, Gregg. What a blessing it was to see them way up on this mountain. Cecil's father, Wayne Lovingood, was a very dear friend of mine. He has now gone on to be with the Lord. Thank God for sending them up here. "Well glory!"

I am sure I will see them again someday in heaven. It's always a blessing to see acquaintances from time to time.

An Experience of Glory in the Mountains

I am sitting by a nice campfire. The flames are beautiful and orange-mingled with some blue with deep red coals beneath white ashes spread around with some wood smoking. Black smoke is trailing upward into a clear blue sky. The air is crisp with an aroma of wild flowers blooming nearby. Birds are singing. I can hear Snowbird Creek cascading down over the rugged rocks. This is music to my ears. I know that out there in the creek there is some mountain trout lurking in the whirling pools; some no doubt that we will eat for supper tonight.

I can also smell another aroma as I sip on a hot cup of coffee. I can smell bacon and tenderloin frying. My two precious sons are doing the cooking. My youngest son, Tony, who is a Director of Medical Imaging for Wellstar, Inc. in Marietta, GA is the chief cook and my oldest son, Dan, who is President of Mars Hill College, is the chief dishwasher and assistant cook. My responsibility is to set by the campfire and eat. Fourteen years ago, I said to my boys, "We need to spend some time together. Suppose you fellows schedule a camping trip, so we can have some quality time together." So they did.

Now, we have been enjoying this outing for fourteen years. What a blessing this is from God. I now am eighty-three years old. For the past several years, I have thought this year may well be the last year I will be able to do this but God continues year after year to make it possible for me to be involved.

We sit around the campfire and talk about many things. We laugh together and pray together. God continues to visit the campfire setting.

One thing that it always does is rain. It is very dry and dusty this time, but just now I heard a clap of thunder in a distance. I have a feeling we may get a much-needed shower. That, too, would be a blessing from God.

At my age now, I just can't do the things I did when I was much younger, like wade the cool mountain streams while fly-fishing. Through the years, I have been an avid trout fisherman. I can't get around over the slick rocks anymore, but God has allowed me to keep some very precious memories. I now am thinking. Going back many years ago, I was camping out with my friends, Ross Cornwell, and Ed Deweese who have long since gone on to be with the Lord. I am now standing in the rim of a large pool of water. The water is plunging over a huge rock cliff thundering into the pool below, making beautiful white foam. I am spell bound at the beauty and the cool freshness from the mist settling on my brow. I feel the cool water surging around my knees and the cool soothing of the water on my burning feet. Momentarily, it seems to me that I can see the face of Jesus in the shining rock as the water cascades down its rugged surface. Then I remember I am there to fish. I take a look at my fly dangling at the end of my leader, which is attached to the end of my fly line. I blow on the fly to be sure it is good and dry and that it will float, as it should. I flex the rod, getting out the right amount of line, dropping the fly right at the rim of the white foam near the center of the pool and let it drift, watching it with a great amount of expectation. Sure enough, there is a big splash and flash of crimson red. Now a tug on my fly rod, and the real fun begins as he jumps and surges in the crystal clear water. I gradually bring him in and now I hold him in my hand. What a beauty it is, a native Mountain Brook Trout or as it is called commonly, a Speckled Trout or a "Speck." I am now thinking about the aroma of him frying in the pan over the campfire and the delicious flavor found only in a Mountain Speckled Trout.

Now, I hear the voice of my son, Tony. "Dad! Breakfast is ready. Come on and get it." My dream ends and I enjoy a breakfast of bacon, tenderloin, eggs, grits, and homemade apple butter with toast browned on the grill.

God is so good all the time. His grace is extended to us in all of life. What more could I ask for. "Well glory...I am glad I am a child of the King."

I hear the voice of Jesus calling out to His weary fishermen disciples when they had toiled all night and caught nothing, "Come and dine." John 21:12. At Jesus' command, they had caught one hundred and fifty-three fish, but Jesus called them to come and eat of the one hundred and fifty-forth fish that they had not caught. He invites us to come and dine on that which He has prepared for us. It is not man's provision, but God's own doing. He wants to bless us with abundant spiritual blessings.

CELEBRATING GOD'S WONDERFUL BLESSINGS WITH FRIENDS

The decade of the nineties had a lot of surprises. I retired as Director of Missions in 1990. That same year, my mother went on to be with the Lord at the age of eighty three. Four years later, my dad also departed this life and we lost three sister-in-laws in death while Gladys had a brother and a nephew who went on to be with the Lord. In 1995, I had a heart attack, spending some time in the hospital and my wife had to have major surgery. During all of this, God manifested Himself to us in ways beyond imagination with blessings to behold.

March 17, 1994, Gladys and I celebrated our Fiftieth Wedding Anniversary. Our boys, Dan and Tony, both live away, so they had to have help to put a Fiftieth Celebration together for us. Karen Twiss, who is Administrative Assistant in the Truett Baptist Association of Churches office, her twin sister, Sharon Kephart, and Glady's niece, Helen Wilson, did the work necessary to pull off this big event. Sharon was working with me for the North Carolina Baptist State Convention.

The Fiftieth Celebration was held at the Truett Baptist Association Center Conference Room. The place was decorated to the peak of awesome beauty. A huge cake was baked and abundant food was provided for everyone. The word was spread by all means available and people came from everywhere to pay their respect and share in our celebration.

We thank God for so many dedicated, loving, friends that allow God to channel His love for us through them.

CELEBRATING SIXTY YEARS

While serving as Pastor of Vengeance Creek Baptist Church, Gladys and I reached an unusual milestone in life. We celebrated our Sixtieth Wedding Anniversary on March 17, 2004.

Gladys' nieces, Nancy Huffines and Helen Wilson, along with several of the godly ladies of the church put on a Sixtieth Wedding Anniversary Event in the Fellowship Hall of the church. A big cake was baked, food was prepared, and the place was decorated to the height of explicit beauty. Invitations went out and people came from far and near along with our boys and their families.

Pictures were taken, and gifts were presented by the scores. Blessings were beyond measure. I thank God for friends and loved ones and their expressions of love.

God is love, so says the Word of God. All people have the ability to become a channel of God's love to others. God is still extending His marvelous grace to us. I am writing this on our sixty-fifth anniversary.

Finishing My Course

The Apostle Paul says in II Timothy 4:7-"I have fought a good fight, I have finished my course."

In the work of association missions, I finished my course at the age of sixty-five in March of 1990. The association planned a big retirement celebration for Gladys and myself. People came from far and near to pay tribute to us. My good friend and fellow Pastor, Rev. Chester Jones, took my place as Director of Missions. Under his leadership, the good people of Cherokee and Clay Counties bought us a car. God surely blessed me with some of the greatest people in the world as co-workers in the Kingdom of God. I shall always be grateful to God for them and their love and friendship. "Well Glory-to His Wonderful Name!"

THE SOUND OF MANY WATERS

The Apostle John was exiled on the Isle of Patmos for his faith. He was in the Spirit on the Lord's day and heard the voice of God speaking to him. "And I turned to see the voice that spake with me. And being turned, I saw seven golden candlesticks, one like unto the Son of man, clothed with a garment down to the foot, and girt about the paps with a golden girdle. His head and His hairs were white like wool, as white as snow: and His eyes were as a flame of fire; and His feet like unto fine brass, as if they burned in a furnace; and His voice as the sounds of many waters."- Revelation 1:12-15.

The voice of many waters can always be heard from the bubbling spring coming from a solid rock on the crest of a majestic mountain peak to the churning, dashing, waves of the ocean and all in between.

John, being in exile on the Isle of Patmos many miles away from his homeland, was lonely and forsaken and left to die. As far as he could see in all directions, was the angry churning sea. The haunting sound of the ocean waves was his to endure day and night. They were a reminder of his plight as he was separated from those whom he loved, but the voice of God was not just the ocean sounds, but the sound of many waters. This voice was as soothing and comforting as a small trickling brook.

One day, my oldest son, Dan and I were fishing a cool mountain stream for lurking Mountain Trout. Lunchtime came and we sat down by a whirling pool that was fed by a surging waterfall. We retrieved our vienna sausage, pork and beans, and saltine crackers from our jacket pockets and prepared to eat. I said, "Let's have a prayer of thanks for our food," and he agreed. We bowed our heads and removed our hats and talked to our Heavenly Father, but we also heard the voice of Him who made the beautiful, cool, mountain, stream and the warm sunshine that was so brilliantly shining upon us while the cool mountain breeze cooled our brows. When we had finished praying, I looked over at him and saw a tear trickling down his face and he said, "Dad, this is the most peaceful place I have ever seen." It was the trickling sound of the water and the beauty of this cool, clear, pool with a center of bubbling, white, foam. I thought, "That is just the way God is." He is the provider of our every need. Here is a young man who is an educator, the Superintendent of a large school system with all the necessary training to do his job that brings with it all of the pressures of running a system of learning. He was sitting high in the mountains by the side of a mountain stream, while the God of the heavens, and earth spoke to his heart with the voice of many waters.

Many times in my life, God has spoken to my heart in so many different ways just like the sound of many waters. It was just the right sound at the right time to meet the needs of my heart. "Well glory!"

GOD IS STILL MOVING IN A MIGHTY WAY

In this second edition of <u>Glory in the Mountains</u>, I will try to share a little of what God has done since writing the last pages of the first edition.

After God's undeniable call to the ministry in 1949, I had the privilege of preaching in many places, even before I was ordained on September 24, 1950.

Now for a little over a year, I have been celebrating God's blessing of sixty years of ministry. In July of 1950, I went to Friendship Baptist Church at Hiawassee, GA for the first time to preach. I had the distinct privilege of going back there on July 18 of this year, 2010, to preach a few days of revival with my dear friend of many years, the present Pastor, Rev. Jimmy Rogers. This was an outstanding blessing from God.

Then, just a few days ago, I was able to see my dear friend and neighbor saved by the grace of God at the age of seventy-three. I have been praying for him for many years. God is still in the blessing business. "Well glory!"

Then, just yesterday, I had the blessed privilege of preaching in New Hope Baptist Church in Graham County. This was the first church I preached in at Graham County sixty years ago.

God blessed in the service by manifesting Himself in such a marvelous way. My wife and I had the glorious opportunity of having lunch in the home of our dear friend of many years, Lerora McCraye. She invited another dear friend, Sue Millsaps, to come be with us. These dear ladies are certainly outstanding Christian sisters. Both of their husbands have gone on to be with the Lord. It was my honor to have a part on their funeral service.

God really blesses beyond measure.

Alphabetical Listing of Names Used in Book

Adams, N. L.

Alan, Helen

Bailey, Jessie

Barker, Robert

Bristol, Aline

Brown, Julia

Buchanan, Faye

Carringer, Bertha

Carringer, Luther

Carringer, Lyle

Carter, Ken

Christy, Jean

Clark, John

Clarke, Dr. Dumont

Clayton, Bill

Clouse, Jim

Cook, Calvin

Cook, Donald

Cook, Francis

Cook, Theodore

Cooper, Maurice

Cornwell, Oliver

Cornwell, Ross

Couch, Mable

Crisp, Melvin

Denton, J. Y.

Deweese, Ed

Deweese, Flonnie

Deweese. Ralph

Dowdle, Thad

Fair, Gene

Fritz, Chaplain

Frye, Lisa

Gaither, Bill

Galloway, Josephine

Gernert, S. J.

Graham, Willard

Graves, Ed

Greene, Elmer

Greene, John

Greene, Willard

Guffey, Marvin

Hardin, L. B.

Hawk, Harry

Hayes, Kate

Hendrix, Garland

Hensley, Oscar

Herbert, Fred

Hicks, Martha

Hogan, Pappy Bert

Hogsed, Lawrence

Hogsed, Ray

Holloway, Glen

Hudson, Isham B.

Huffines, Nancy

Hughes, Dan

Hunsucker, Homer

James, Frank

Jones, Alec

Jones, Chester

Jones, Cora

Kephart, Don

Kephart, Frank

Kephart, Josephine

Kephart, Ralph

Kephart, Sharon

King, Grady

King, Iva Lee

King, Wylie
Logan, Jane
Logan, June
Long, Lucy
Lovell, A. B
Lovin, Jack
Lovingood, Cecil
Lovingood, Cooter
Lovingood, Gregg
Lovingood, Paul
Lovingood, Wayne
Lunsford, Dan
Lunsford, Furel
Lunsford, Gladys Greene
Lunsford, Hoyt
Lunsford, Inez Rogers
Lunsford, Natalie
Lunsford, Pearlie
Lunsford, Tony
Matheson, Ralph
McAuliffe, Anthony
McConnell, Buck
McConnell, Doris
McRae, Jim
McCraye, Lerora
Miller, Harold
Millsaps, Sue
Morris, J. Alton
Mosteller, Lenora
Myers, Betty
Myers, Daisy
Myers, Marion
Myers, Ralph
Newman, John
O'Dell, Octavia
Palmer, Barbara
Palmer, Derrick
Palmer, Ronnie

Patton, General George
Payne, Loy
Payne, Max
Phillips, Charlie
Phillips, Grant
Pittman, Buddy
Powers, Richard
Rogers, Ellen King
Rogers, Jimmy
Rogers, Uncle Doc
Rogers, Will
Rose, Beatrice
Rose, Brian
Rose, Bruce
Rose, Jr., Frank
Rose, Kendal
Scruggs, Gordon
Senator Miligan
Sexton, Charlie
Shuler, Ronnie
Smart, Dr.
Smith, Jim
Stewart, Daniel
Stewart, Robert
Sutton, Guy
Tanner, William
Taylor, Roy
Townson, Freed
Truett, George W.
Turner, Don
Twiss, Karen Kephart
Vaught, Jim
Walker, Suthell
Ware, Rex
Wiley, Robert
Wilson, Helen ,
Zimmerman, Edith
Zimmerman, Elizabeth

ABOUT THE AUTHOR

Fred Lunsford has been one of God's choice patriarchs since his humble ministry began some six decades ago in North Georgia and Western North Carolina. He is and always has been an aggregate of personal achievement, the essence of moral character, and the embodiment of Christian commitment and devotion. He has served churches, large and small, too numerous to mention, but each faithfully and fruitfully. No church has ever been forgotten or left behind.

Even in times between pastorates and some retirement, fresh ideas and projects continued to emerge. Refusing to grow old, he remains young in mind and heart with the same commitment and freshness as when he first began.

During his brief stay at Robbinsville First Baptist Church, he launched the Lighthouse Ministries, designed to promote growth in the small congregations in the mountain area. I still proudly wear his lighthouse lapel pin from time to time. He also initiated the annual journey with local pastors and other church leaders to the mountains in and around Hooper Bald. Prior to the holy pilgrimage, the group always meets for a prayer breakfast at one of the local churches. They always pause at various intervals to have prayer especially standing upon a large symbolic landmark rock of faith. Brother Fred has been known to recall how he hesitated to reach his hands outward and upward lest he touch the face of our Lord. A lesser man of faith would have made excuses before undertaking such a strenuous endeavor, but the patriarch of the mountains seemed to say, "God, give me another mountain to climb. Lift me up to a higher plain that I may walk on heaven's table lands."

The spiritual impact, which he has had on the tri-state area, cannot be adequately described or measured. His preaching and teaching has brought great blessings to himself and to the entire region. One of his trademarks as the Spirit is overflowing is his simple exclamation, "Well glory!" The entire mountain region in unison says, "Keep telling the Story."

Jack P. Lovin Robbinsville, N. C.

LaVergne, TN USA
30 November 2010

206692LV00002B/4/P